RESIDUE

Surviving and Overcoming the Stains of
Generational Curses and Soul Ties

Debbie L. London

First Edition: March 2017

10 9 8 7 6 5 4 3 2 1

ISBN-10:0-692-86088-6

ISBN-13:978-0-692-86088-5

Convalesce Publishing
P.O. Box 1158
Dallas, GA 30132

debbiellondon.com

This book is dedicated to my son and daughter. May they never have to deal with the baggage of my past because that link has been broken with me.

PREFACE

Generational curses and soul ties are like hand-me-down clothing continuously passed from one person to the next. Slugs leave a residue everywhere they go. The process of creating the stain is slow, but once it's there, it's difficult to remove. Sometimes the stains go unnoticed but definitely present themselves later. This is what the cover of the book illustrates. These stains can be thought of as the many links in the chain of generational curses and soul ties. Think about the problems that you have in your life and where they have come from. Have you—knowingly or unknowingly—received an old tattered shirt covered with stains from someone before you? Did you, perhaps, receive a stained garment from a previous lover while in a toxic relationship?

This book is sure to assist you with peeling back the layers of your life, identify the generational curses and soul ties, and finally releasing yourself from the residue of the past. I always wondered why I experienced the things I went through and witnessed growing up. My curiosity and bewilderment then led me to take an interest in psychology. I wanted to have a better understanding of why people were the way they were. Seeing sexual abuse, absent fathers (even those physically present in the home), sexism, physical abuse, misogyny, among other things, in my very own family shaped who I was and brought me to where I am. I finally gained understanding when I realized the things that I experienced were the result of unchecked generational curses.

Years ago, God placed it on my heart to write about generational curses and their effects on the people plagued by them. A lot of my questions were answered with God's help and the encouragement of my support system. Healing began to take place once I understood generational curses and soul ties. My prayer is that this book will help unlock issues that have been plaguing you so that you can uproot what should no longer be a part of your life. Additionally, we will cover soul ties. Soul ties and generational curses are deeply correlated. Generational curses beget soul ties and vice versa, because that unresolved soul tie then transforms you and you pass it on to others. Generational curses are powerful forces (if we allow them to be) that can ruin our lives and the lives of those who come after us if we don't sever the link. I must warn you that parts of this book will be uncomfortable because you will be taken through my journey and my life. Discomfort is necessary, though, in order to help us take an introspective look at our lives and unshackle ourselves from the chains that have had us bound. Through this book, I hope to help you identify generational curses, sever the ties, and heal yourself and others.

Pray with me...

Heavenly Father, bless me as I read this book. Break every generational curse and soul tie that has attached itself to me. Let the cycle stop with me. Protect the generations after me from the residue left from those before me. Give me peace and freedom, mentally, emotionally, spiritually, and physically, heal me in all the broken areas of my life (known and unknown). Give me the discernment and wisdom necessary to navigate my life and make sound decisions. Grant me the boldness to pass the healing on to others. In Jesus Name, Amen!

HARMLESS HAND-ME-DOWNS

A hand-me-down is an article of clothing or item that has been passed on to someone else. Generational curses and soul ties can be considered types of hand-me-downs that we sometimes don't even realize we have inherited.

INTRODUCTION

AT THE TIME OF WRITING THIS, I am 29 years old; married for over two years with two little munchkins. So far in my short life, I have witnessed sexual, physical, verbal, and emotional abuse within my own family. I have personally endured two second trimester miscarriages, a failed business, an abortion, terrible relationships, struggles with identity, spiritual conflicts, bankruptcy, phony friendships, ridiculous family members, and becoming the product of generational curses and soul ties.

Now, some of you may ask how I could be qualified to speak on the topic of generational curses and soul ties. Well, you will soon find out as you move forward in the book. Experience is truly the best teacher. The chaos within my family created within me a yearning to understand why people are the way they are and how they can heal from it.

I studied psychology in college because I thought I would be a psychologist one day. However, working in the field after I graduated completely turned me off because there was too much red tape preventing me from helping people, and I didn't want to be confined to rules. So, I ditched my master's program for professional counseling and got my master of public administration instead.

As much as I tried to get away from mental health, I always ended up coming back to it somehow. Whether I was giving close friends, family, or even strangers the word they needed or peeling back the layers of my own life, mental health found its way back to me. It is really a God-given gift to be able to talk others through their issues and discern what is going on through a powerful mixture of spiritual sensitivity and personal experiences.

This is why I'm here to help you. God instructed me years ago to write about generational curses and their effects. However, I was disobedient and felt terrified of the idea of sharing my life story in an effort to help others. The nakedness was too much for me. Honestly, as I am writing I am still a little terrified because I have never been so vulnerable before. It's not about me, though; it's all about you. Everything I've endured has been for you. Nothing we ever go through is for us; it is always to help the next person. This moment was meant to be, and healing is the goal. You ready?

CHAPTER 1

What Is a Generational Curse and Soul Tie?

BEFORE WE GET INTO ANYTHING ELSE, we must define generational curses (GCs) and soul ties (STs). These are my personal definitions, so walk with me. GCs are inherited negative links (i.e. behaviors, addictions, mentalities, or attitudes) passed down from a previous generation. GCs can also be additional links created in an attempt not to fall prey to an ever-present GC in one's own family. Typically, the links are direct from parent to child but that is not always the case.

In my family, some of the generational curses are sexual abuse, lack of follow through, the victim mentality, physical/emotional/verbal abuse, and inability or refusal to move forward from traumatic events. What are some of the generational curses in your family? Have you inherited any? *Write them down and do a self-evaluation so you know where you are with this.*

As I mentioned, another branch of GCs arises when you create a new GC in an effort not to become what you despise. For example, I became extremely prideful and felt the need to prove others wrong in an effort to avoid becoming the victim of my circumstances. My relationships were with people I felt I could control to an extent, and this faux wall of strength started to appear. I will delve more into that later. I just wanted to make it clear that generational curses can be passed down or created by circumstance or hurt that hasn't been healed. GCs can take form psychologically or spiritually.

Now, as an African American, generational curses are really nothing new for me. They transcend all races and backgrounds, but I want to give another example of what a generational curse is and how it can develop. If you are not familiar with the Willie Lynch Letter, please take a moment to go to the appendix of this book for the link to read it, like now. It may be hard a read for some, but it is a classic example of how generational curses form. Unfortunately, there were no lies told in this letter about how to create a slave for generations. Although this letter is considered a hoax, the content is still relevant. Some of the very issues I touch on in this book about my life and the people in it are outlined in this letter. In my own family, the issues of weak men and strong women, colorism (prejudice or discrimination, typically among people of the same ethnic or racial group, against individuals with a dark skin tone), the shattered female, the broken marriage, and so forth are prevalent.

It is scary to say, but the methods discussed in the Willie Lynch letter worked. The generational curses in the black community are evident, and the letter really brings home enslaving people not just physically but mentally, emotionally, and spiritually for generations to come. Additionally, the ideologies of racist people who see blacks as inferior constitute a generational curse. That mentality was passed down and taught just like any other generational curse.

At this particular time, racism is being shoved in the faces of many who can't and won't believe that it exists. Some believe that because we are in the 21st century, racism has somehow disappeared, which is far from the truth. Now the reason it is a generational curse is because it is not natural behavior to hate someone for the color of his or her skin. Hate is a learned behavior.

My son is in preschool and his best friend is white. They genuinely love each other, which is the way it's supposed to be. It's not until the ideology that was passed down from someone's great- great-great-great-great-grandfather reaches the current generation that hate resumes. Because granddaddy said blacks were bad and lesser, now you have to believe that, too. Now, due to that continuous hate and purposeful naivety, black and other non-white people are always on guard and feel belittled in certain environments.

Regardless of the status, accomplishments, or good works of so many black people in America, there are people who will ALWAYS see blacks as inferior and who will seek to discount them. All of this over skin color. With the police brutalities that seem to target black men and minorities, there is always someone somewhere justifying the death of someone else at the hands of these law enforcement officers. It is a sad and unfortunate reality, at least until other people acknowledge our struggle and band together to stop the generational curse of hatred. There are people of other backgrounds who acknowledge our struggle and who have joined with us to stop the generational curse of hatred. I pray their numbers continue to increase. The same needs to happen with the attitudes of black people about ourselves. If we all come together, regardless of our color or backgrounds, and vow to break the chains of racism and prejudice, can you imagine the peace that we would have? Wow, the thought of that type of unity gives me chills.

Again, this book is for all backgrounds and people; I just wanted to provide another solid example of a generational curse to assist you with perspective as you read this book and evaluate your own life. HOWEVER, I truly believe that if you are ready, exhausted from being in the cycle, and want to be free finally, you can break the curses in your own life and assist others who are ready to do the same.

A soul tie is a connection in spirit through sexual intercourse. Soul ties are negative. This is why it is important to guard your temple (body) and be selective in who you lay with because you don't know the spiritual baggage the other person is carrying. Soul ties are similar to GCs, but the difference is these are inherited issues or, perhaps more illuminating, demons from a partner. Have you ever changed your behavior dramatically for the worse once you started dating someone? For instance, you never smoked or dabbled in drugs; yet, now you suddenly do. Your lifestyle has changed to mirror your partner's. Maybe you were focused and ambitious, but now you are dating someone who isn't. You have suddenly lost all motivation to accomplish your goals. These are examples of how soul ties reveal themselves outwardly. They can also manifest themselves internally. Every person you sleep with is another attachment. Whoever you lay with in addition to who they have been with becomes an intertwined mess of spiritual toxicity. If you were able to use a spiritual microscope to see what the person you have sex with is carrying, would you still do it? We should use the spiritual microscopes that are available to us —wisdom and discernment—to have the appropriate kinds of relationships with people.

My first undeniable experience with a soul tie was during my college years. I was attracted to the wrong guys for the wrong reasons. That is the plight of most young women (and men, too) on the dating scene. I realized that I had a type: weak-minded guys without a sense of direction in their lives who were momma's boys. Now this is not to say that I was without flaws because I had my own baggage; being insecure was one of my major problems. In my subconscious, I liked these types because I felt (emphasis on felt) like I "ran" the relationship since I was ambitious and focused. In actuality, I wasn't doing anything but trying to force these young men to fit into boxes that did not fit them. Each time, in the end, we both wound up hurt.

Now that we have briefly defined what generational curses and soul ties are, take a moment to bring your guard down and ruminate on your life and experiences. You are reading this for a reason. I truly believe that if these concepts didn't apply to your life in some way, you wouldn't be reading this book. The links are being severed already because you have taken the first of many steps to your healing.

DEFINITIONS RECAP

At the end of every section, there will be a short exercise to help you in your journey of healing. I recommend writing the questions and your answers down in a journal. Writing always brings the mirror of your life up close so that you can see the areas that need improvement.

1. Now that you have a better idea of what generational curses and soul ties are, how do you define them?
2. Do you have any experience (directly or indirectly) with either GCs or STs? If so, list those experiences.
3. Are there any hand-me-downs that you have acquired due to GCs and STs?
4. List the ways those experiences hinder you mentally, emotionally, and spiritually.

SEEING STAINS

We have all received a piece of clothing from someone at some point in our lives. After close examination, we notice blatant and maybe some not so obvious stains. The same happens in our own lives as we start to notice our unique personality flaws and behaviors. Where did these stains come from?

CHAPTER 2:

Identifying the Curses and Ties

S O, I HAVE TO GIVE a little background about the people you
will hear about the most throughout this book. Bear with me as I
will be giving condensed snapshots to clarify who we are dealing
with. You will hear the most about my grandfather, Uncle Ellis, Uncle
Matt, my mother, and my grandmother. These people have
absolutely shaped my life. Some for the worse, some for my
betterment, and some are a mixture of the two.

At one point in my life, I was the black sheep of my family
because certain family members were hell-bent on singling me out
all the time. Maybe you will find them similar to people you know or
to some of your family members. Most of the stories I share are

heavy and others may seem not to be as serious to some readers. I wanted to ensure that I not only touched on the heavy stuff but also what would appear to be an insignificant event to show how things can shape who we are. No matter how big or small the life event, it is <u>huge</u> part of your story. We tend to discount the small things when they, too, are most significant. Also, don't mistake my passionate tone as evidence that I am still bothered by these events. I just wanted to make sure you could feel where I was coming from in those moments. I have healed and released these events in my life; otherwise, I wouldn't be able to share them with you so freely.

Additionally, I do not consider myself a religious person, at least not anymore, but I am definitely a spiritual person. I am extremely sensitive to God's voice. Those subtle nudges to relay a message to someone or to do something have always been a part of my life. I used to question if I heard His voice or if I was getting His voice confused with my own. As I have matured in my spiritual journey, He has confirmed time and time again that it was indeed His voice I was hearing. I try my best to be obedient every time God instructs me to do something, no matter how uncomfortable it makes me to do as He asked. Most times my obedience is crucial for someone else. In other words, I have to do what He says no matter how I feel about it because someone else's peace, clarity, or whatever he or she needs is dependent on me being obedient in that moment. For example, writing this book was very uncomfortable for me; but writing it was never about me or my comfort level; it is about freeing you.

I make references to prayer and connecting with God throughout this book. I am all about connection to God and direct communication with Him. We are all spiritual beings in physical shells in a physical realm. The stories I share with you about some family members, even those that recount negative situations or experiences, highlight that we are spiritual beings and remind us that we aren't wrestling with the people themselves but the negative spirits within them (Ephesians 6:12-13). Just like some people seem to be angels on earth because they can literally be a breath of fresh air with just their presence, others can seem to be devils in thinly veiled disguises.

Everyone's religious and spiritual background is different, and I truly respect that. In my journey, I needed God to get through everything. Sometimes church wasn't there, scripture wouldn't do it, but hearing from Him directly got me through it. I am not a Bible beater or someone trying to convert anyone to anything, but from my view, believing in God is essential to getting through life's struggles. I have always been able to hear His voice, even in my darkest hours. Though I questioned it when it happened to me, I was able to hear Him comforting me and directing me. I do not have a secret formula for hearing from God, but I believe that having faith in Him and being open to Him are important first steps on the road to full healing.

Removing the expectation of a certain response and allowing Him to communicate with you in His own way is also helpful. When I am unable to hear from Him, it is normally because I want a specific response in a certain way. But that's not how God works. I would throw tantrums when I didn't get my way spiritually, which is, of course, spiritual (as well as life) immaturity. I have learned to communicate with Him about everything, be open to His responses, and do my part by being obedient to Him. Just be! That means do all that you can do on your end and allow God to do the rest and move in your life. This frees you up emotionally and mentally because once you have done all that you can, you are trusting God to take on what you cannot do and believing by faith that He will. Some of you have been through utter hell. I want to encourage you not to give up. I pray that these experiences I am sharing with you give you hope and the courage to turn things around for the better. We have all been tired, all been defeated, wondered what we have to live for, why we have had to endure so much, and so on. You are not alone in this. Don't give up! Let's start healing!

CHAPTER 3:

The Beginning

I REMEMBER DISTINCTLY BEING three years old and hearing the loud yells and screams erupt in my grandparents' house. Dishes were breaking, belittling things were being said. This was the first time I started to form opinions about those closest to me and from there, my skewed view on life was born. My grandfather was and has always been a hothead of sorts. More than that, he has a twisted perception of love and what it means to show it. He believes that since he is the provider of the home financially that means he is entitled to do whatever he pleases even at the expense of everyone else.

My grandmother, mother, and uncles suffered the most at the hands of my grandfather. I watched my grandmother get berated constantly and torn down by a man who claimed to love her and honor her. She went back and forth on whether or not she would divorce him, allowed trauma to happen to her own children, endured cheating, all in the name of security and the life to which she had grown accustomed. Maybe she didn't feel strong enough to separate from him.

I love an good old school love story, but at what point was enough, *enough*? I remember that, after one of their many disputes, my grandmother noticed me watching her, and I was speechless from what she had just endured. She looked at me and said, "he wasn't always this way. He used to write me love letters." At the time, I didn't understand what the heck that had to do with anything. This man just told you that you weren't worth anything (insert bad language) and you are trying to smooth it over by romanticizing who he used to be? Naw, I was not buying it. These were my thoughts as a young child, but those incidents also taught me a terrible lesson: it is acceptable for a man to treat you this way as long as he once showed you good qualities because maybe one day he will be that way again (insert face palm).

I didn't realize watching the matriarch and patriarch of my family in their volatile, loveless, disrespectful relationship would mold me the way that it did, but I was an innocent bystander, unaware that I was receiving hand-me-downs against my will and without my knowledge. This is also why it is extremely important that parents are careful with how they act and what they expose their children to. Of course, arguments, disagreements, giving space when needed, compromise and other normal aspects of a relationship will occur. Sadly, abuse of any kind is observed by the little people in your life, who interpret such behavior as normal. Parents and caretakers must be careful not to open another doorway for generational curses to creep in and change the direction of their children's lives.

I was around women who were docile, had no voice, and had no vision of their own. They intentionally turned a blind eye to serious matters that were happening to and around them to avoid accountability or having to make decisions for their betterment. Watching them caused me to create a faux sense of strength. I was so disturbed by the way they allowed men to treat them that as a child, I felt I had to do the opposite. I was loud, opinionated, and, more than anything, determined that I would not be run over. I was told I was sassy, should tone down my attitude, and be more lady like. This rhetoric mainly came from the abusive men in my family; go figure. Of course, you don't want me to speak up for myself because that would leave you powerless against me. Sometimes I think that because I was so outspoken, I somehow protected myself from being physically and sexually abused. Perhaps they knew that if they ever attempted to do anything, I would sound the alarm immediately.

Some of my uncles are still suffering from the effects of my grandfather's harsh parenting tactics. I used his negative banter as fuel to prove that I would do whatever I set out to do whether I succeeded or failed. Follow through is another issue in my family. I define follow through as doing everything you say you will do instead of merely talking about it. Unfortunately, the victim mentality has caused a frozen like state for some of my relatives due to how they were treated. Everyone handles trauma differently; some people are able to pull themselves up and move past it, while others cannot. This is why I am a huge advocate of counseling and mental health care. It is unfortunate that people cannot seem to get past the victim mentality so that they can be healed and do the things they want to do. In a perfect world, I would make my whole family go to group and individual counseling so they can finally heal; but I know that won't happen.

Black people in particular can be anti-mental health and pro prayer. We need both to get the full healing that's needed. It is my belief that prayer requires action on our part and allowing God to do what He does during the process. Now that I am a mother, I am still healing from knowing that people in my bloodline sexually abused their children. I still struggle with this because I will kill anyone who tries to bring harm to my babies. I have less than a handful of people I trust to watch our children for us. My kids aren't yet at the age to articulate for themselves, and I want them to be in trustworthy hands. We are all a work in progress. I know it is not right to have such a distrust of people; but, especially when it comes to my children, I want to be hyper vigilant.

My grandfather and other men constantly told me what I wasn't going to be and that I was headed down the wrong path. My mother felt I was strong enough to handle things on my own, so she was never really present with me emotionally. I used those negative things that haunted me throughout my life to push me through high school, graduate from college, get my master's degree, and start a career in mental health. Guess what? None of that even mattered because I was using material possessions like my BMW (that was voluntarily repossessed), living in Buckhead (an affluent area in Atlanta...with a roommate), accumulating mounds of debt (to buy crap I didn't need) to maintain a lifestyle just to give the middle finger to the people who said I couldn't do it. That worked out poorly. Material things and titles were very important to me at that time in my life. I used them to fill voids to make me feel complete, important, and worthy. Sometimes we use things to insulate ourselves from the pain in our lives because at the time it seems easier to use a coping mechanism than to face it and heal. For you it could be drugs, sex, achievement, etc. Remember, no matter how much you try to mask the pain eventually it will all come to the surface. The choice is yours whether to continue living a lie or face your demons and annihilate them.

Do you know who you are, truly?

CHAPTER 4:

Family Matters

IT WAS INTERESTING GROWING up with people who claimed to be devout Christians. I consider myself a Christian, but I am more focused on the personal relationship that I have with God and Christ rather than the formalities associated with church life and religion. I am all about loving others and being the best person that I can be. God and I are currently on a journey together where I am in a re-discovery phase of my life.

In my grandparent's household, we went to Sunday School and church every single Sunday, in addition to any other services held at our church. In hindsight, I wonder how in the world can you possibly shove church down the throats of everyone around you, but then so blatantly refuse to follow the very principles that you claim to live by. It really annoys me in general when Christians pick and choose what scriptures to follow or want to be hard on others about the way they live their lives without examining their own. For example, if I were to disrespect my mother I would get the "honor your mother and father" scripture thrown in my face. However, this admonition would come from a man who fondles his own daughter and beats his wife...interesting.

To this very day, my grandfather claims to be Christian, goes to a southern Baptist church that he absolutely hates and causes discord in, grimaces at the name of Christ; yet, wants people to take him seriously when he offers life advice. My grandfather is a living example of the fact that we are just spirit beings in physical shells. When we run into people we don't vibe with or the energy is off or no matter what somehow, we always end up in drama through our interactions with them, that is a negative spirit causing the discord. It goes the same way if there is someone who oozes optimism, positivity, and lightheartedness. That is a positive spirit. I have personally seen my grandfather go in and out between the demon that has attached itself to him and himself. Literally, his voice changes and you know when you are speaking directly to the demon. I know that certain life events have happened to him to cause him to live over eight decades and still be as bitter and ornery as ever with no sign of him shedding his hardened heart.

He was 18 and overseas when his mother passed away. This is one event that I know he still carries with him. The guilt he feels that he was not there for her, he wasn't able to say goodbye via the funeral, and was inaccessible due to being in the military. This is a hurt that he hasn't dealt with. Maybe this was the key event that caused him to morph into the malevolent person he is today. He has not mentioned his father ever, and when you ask about him, he gets defensive. It is impossible to communicate with my grandfather, even if it is a lighthearted conversation. It is the epitome of walking through a mine field. What I do know is that he hasn't always been this way and that something happened and events took place in his life that led to him being an abusive father and husband and an overall negative person in general. I can't help but think that somewhere deep inside of him that he wants to change but he has been a host to this demon for so long that now he probably feels like it is who he is, when it's not. However, he has chosen to live a life of pandemonium time and time again.

In addition to my grandfather being a strong negative force in my life there was also an uncle who insisted on tearing me down every moment he got a chance to: my Uncle Ellis. Nowadays, we have had enough battles that he knows not to cross the line with me anymore. But when I was a child, he wanted to silence me by tearing me down. He couldn't do what he had done to his wife and children—intimidate them and abuse them physically—so he chose verbal abuse and manipulation in an attempt to gain control of me. Fortunately, he failed, and I thank God that even when I was a child He gave me discernment and wisdom even when I didn't completely understand what was going on.

When I was 12 years old, this uncle of mine accused me of being a whore because I had taken an interest in boys. As we were riding in a car, I noticed a boy walking along the street, and I said, "he's cute." Nothing more; nothing less. He went on a complete tirade about how I don't need to worry about boys and so on—not in the normal, concerned parent way, but in a psycho irrational manner. As a preteen, it is pretty normal to start noticing the opposite sex. For him, it was further ammunition to run his "Anti-Debbie Campaign."

I was branded the black sheep of my family because for no reason apparent to me, I was targeted for all kinds of nonsense. You have to realize that when people see your strength and they are weak themselves, they will do all that they can to strip you down to bring you to their level. Due to this albatross I was now wearing around my neck, I was never able to spend time with my cousins outside of their parents' supervision. I was labeled a bad influence, and I was considered a threat because I had a voice. Because I have a lighter skin tone than some of my relatives, though I consider myself a regular brown, I soon became aware that a few of the men in my family have a colorism issue. Apparently, lighter skin is seen as more desirable and some of the men in my family automatically felt the need to be harder on me due to my skin tone. For example, if you had lighter skin that meant that boys would be an issue sooner because you were seen as more attractive. Therefore, the men felt that you had to be more carefully watched and sheltered than someone with darker skin. It is so sickening because as African Americans, we are already divided with crap like this. For those same views to be passed down in your family is disturbing.

When I was in high school, my closest relative, one of Uncle Ellis's daughters, began attending the same school as me. He would not allow her to stay the night with me because he was certain that I would expose her to some alternative lifestyle like drugs, sex, or boys. At this time, I was a virgin, and to this day, I have never done drugs. We would be under the supervision of my mother, but for my uncle, that shield still wasn't enough because he felt that my mother gave my brother and me too much freedom. Ironically, he would come down on me the hardest, but his harsh parenting drove his children to do errant things. What he feared I would do, he created himself in his own children. As he beat his wife and abused his children, he saw me, a mere 15-year-old, as a threat to his daughters.

CHAPTER 5:

A Mother's Love or Lack Thereof

MY MOTHER NEVER CAME to my defense any time her father or brothers constantly badgered me or accused me of things. Some people will try to control how others view you once they realize that they can't control you directly. Some of my uncles were on a mission to make my mom view me as they did, and they succeeded somewhat.

My mom watched on numerous occasions as my uncles scolded me, and she never came to my defense. She would even look away when I looked to her for protection as I attempted to defend myself in those moments. I would be humiliated that family members were manipulated (by Uncle Ellis) into thinking that I was a wayward child when that wasn't true, as my mom idly stood by and let it happen time and time again. More than that, that I was devastated that my mom would turn the other cheek just as her mother had done to her, though not on the same scale. In these moments, I lost respect for her. I saw her as less than strong for allowing verbal and emotional abuse to happen to her own child. What could I really expect, though, when she was a victim who had not yet healed herself? I didn't realize and couldn't understand that my mom was still a bruised and battered little girl on the inside, still looking for someone to protect her; so how could she protect me effectively? My grandmother didn't protect her when she spent the summers in Pine Mountain, GA, knowing she would be in the presence of an uncle who was a known child molester. My great-grandmother was aware of it too. Where was the protection? Instead, when my mother went to my grandmother after being molested, her response was "oh, he is known to do that." *Are you kidding me?* Your daughter has just revealed to you that she has been molested, worse, by a relative, and that is your only response? No comforting, no vowing to make heads roll, no sense of urgency, absolutely nothing.

The fact that my grandmother was able to ignore her own daughter about something so serious is an indication that this kind of assault had happened to her, and she was only giving the kind of response that she had received. She had been conditioned to turn a blind eye to abuse, and she expected my mother to do the same.

How sad, sick, and twisted is this —from a mother? Unfortunately, this is the reality of many women, and men as well, when it comes to abuse. They have no one to run to because the person they would look to had no one, and so forth…. See the pattern and the trickle-down effect of unhealed wounds? Generational curses at their best.

This wouldn't be the last time my grandmother turned a blind eye to my mother's troubles. My grandparents have eight children; my mother is the only girl. As I have mentioned before, I watched my grandfather force himself on my mother, making her kiss him, grabbing and touching her as she fought him off. *Great memories for a kid.* When I told my mother that I witnessed those things once I became an adult, she shared with me that it had gone on since she was an adolescent and my grandmother was beyond aware of it. She <u>never</u> came to my mother's aid.

My grandmother actually rationalized my grandfather's actions to my mother by telling her things like: "well you looked too much like him"; "we shouldn't have doted on you so much"; "having you in the house was like having another woman in the house"; and "I hoped that once you got older you would move out." No wonder my mother had been incapable of healthy emotional relationships.

She had to become cold to deal with the crap she had been dealt from her own parents and relatives.

Her parents were poor examples of showing her what love was, and from there she had a distorted view and was unable to understand pure intimacy even with my brother and me. In slight defense of my grandmother, my grandfather has always abused my grandmother in one form or another. He used to beat her, which I have also witnessed, and to this day, he still abuses her verbally and emotionally although she has dementia. Maybe fear is why she never had the courage to leave him and protect my mom and her other children. More than anything, her security was more important to her than her happiness, her safety, and her children's well-being.

Some women in my grandmother's time married out of necessity and felt that they couldn't survive on their own no matter what was at stake by them staying. There are some women today who also have this mindset of marrying for security even if it is to the detriment of themselves and everyone around them. The irony in this is that my grandmother stayed with this man who has done so much wrong for security, but now in her 80s, she cannot utilize those funds to get the care that she needs because he is in control of everything. He apparently does not want her last days to be her best. So, all of her heartache and suffering were ultimately for nothing. I truly wish I could have picked her brain before the dementia set in to understand why she allowed so much to happen to herself and her children. I know that love was not the reason. Maybe because she saw what her mother endured, she considered this way of life the norm. My great-grandfather had quite a few outside children while he was married to my great-grandmother. Who knows what else took place in the home in addition to multiple affairs?

CHAPTER 6:

Relationship Issues

THE EVENTS THAT I WITNESSED and that took place in my mother's life ruined my own view on topics such as submission, my role in a relationship, men, trusting people especially family, and other important issues. My jaded perspective also gave birth to an additional link in this cycle of destruction; I just didn't know it. My mother is still scarred from my grandmother's lack of support when she had children.

My grandmother went missing in action instead of rushing to be by my mother's side when she gave birth to me. My grandmother assured my mother that she would figure it out even though she knew my father was neither present nor willing to support my mother. This absence was another blow my mother got from my grandmother. It seems that my grandmother had resentment against her only daughter, and she also felt ashamed that my mother had to have a shotgun wedding. Regardless of the motivation, my grandmother's lack of support was unjustifiable. The theme of jealousy and resentment between mothers and daughters is another issue within my family. This issue is important to think about because what has happened generation after generation has affected me and all those involved.

This is an example of why there are some weak men and strong women with the "I must be independent at all costs" attitude. The men are coddled, and their behavior is reinforced while the women are left out to fend for themselves. A cousin of mine made a great point when she said "as women, we saw that the men in our family were incapable of doing for us, so we decided to take on the role ourselves. In addition, in relationships, these are the types we looked for since that is what we were used to and once we got with REAL men we had to learn how to let them love us and return love back."

My grandfather abused his sons physically. Some were able to heal from it and move forward in their lives; others have been crippled by it, and to this day have not recovered. I am in favor of spanking children, but there is a difference between spanking and outright abuse. I know it's old school to beat your kids, but the line has to be drawn somewhere. It is one thing to spank your children or to use other types of discipline to correct behavior, but punching or inflicting other kinds of violence is completely uncalled for. My grandfather was a ruthless disciplinarian with his children. As a parent, I know that you cannot treat all of your kids the same because some are more sensitive than others. My uncles are classic examples of that. Some of them used his harsh ways to leave home as soon as they could, by way of the military, school, marriage, or other means, and others are still broken down and unable to stand up and be men in their own homes. A couple have become replicas of who my grandfather was. My Uncle Ellis in particular is crippled by my grandfather's abuse and is unable to lead a stable life because he has not dealt with the issues of his past. Instead, he has become the very kind of man who hurt him.

It is truly a tangled, twisted, trickle-down effect of how generational curses scar everyone. Can you imagine, men in their 30s all the way to their 50s unable to have respectful conversations with their father or unable to stand up for themselves because they still harbor their childhood fear of him? What about men who are now husbands who not only suffered abuse themselves, but who abuse their wives in the same manner they witnessed? Or men who have reversed roles in their relationships or marriages and are unable to be the heads of their households because they don't want to be controlling and abusive men like their father? Instead, they prefer to be walked all over by their mates. Strength in a man (or woman) does not equal abuse and control.

Strength is the ability to take care of your household and make the decisions necessary for upward movement with respect and love. Additionally, the damage of being abused runs so deeply with my relatives that they are unable to make sound decisions, not only in relationships but in their personal lives as well. Communication is poor, and the ability to maintain healthy relationships is impossible. They are so used to being manipulated and fearful that they end up doing to others the very things they despise in their abuser.

Do you know anyone like that? When people are sneaky, manipulative and dishonest, chances are they are emulating treatment they have received. I am not excusing behaviors like these, but I believe that more times than not, negative behaviors are learned or adapted. Hopefully, this book will also help you see past people's direct behaviors toward you so that you can keep necessary distance from them while also praying for their healing.

CHAPTER 7:

Poverty of the Mind

THE CYCLE OF POVERTY IS another generational curse. Now I know there are many third world countries that struggle daily with poverty. Even in the US, there is poverty as well. However, I am talking more about the poverty of the mind. Have you seen that in some families there is struggle from one generation to the next, with their finances, in their relationships, due to their attitudes, or other negative behavior?

In my family, due to all of the baggage from the past, struggle and poverty seem to be recurring themes as well. Walk with me here because I am not solely focusing on material things. I mean settling for always having just enough to get by, letting fear keep them from truly following their dreams, never wanting to step foot outside the box, or creating new boxes to entrap themselves and their loved ones.

For example, my grandfather served in the military, and his ultimate goal was to get out of rural southern Georgia, which we call "the country." He believed that there was more for him in the city. So, he left the country, went to the military, returned to southern Georgia, got married, and became a father. While he was on his journey to beat the odds, and exit country life, there were people at home who had doubted him, saying he would never make it. He was able to disprove the naysayers who were reacting in fear towards his goals. However, although he made it out of the country, he carried within him those other voices of doubt and fear. I have come to realize that many times when people treat you a certain way they are doing so to retaliate against those voices within them, and not necessarily against you.

My grandfather looked down on any of my family members who wanted to go to college because my grandfather didn't go to college. He took up a trade instead. Once he got over the fear of going to college, he began to talk down to those who didn't go to a post-secondary school near the family home, but chose instead to branch out within Georgia. Once someone wanted to go out of state to school, he really had a heart attack then, because he didn't think it could be done. From the time I graduated from high school until the day I graduated from college, he gave me hell for going to school in North Carolina. Instead of giving me encouragement, he attacked me with those same words of extreme doubt and fear that he had once heard. Again, poverty of the mind proved to be a strong tradition for him.

Some people will not be able to move forward until they let go of the skeletons of the past. Even though they may have beaten the odds despite the naysayers, they still carry that hurt from the discouragement they endured. Now those same fears are fueled when others also try to beat the odds in their own ways. If the person was healed, he or she would be able to be a catalyst for change and positivity and not try to hold someone back just because someone once tried to hold him or her back. As the saying goes, hurt people *hurt* people.

Another example of poverty from my family is that if anyone did anything good or upgraded in anyway my grandfather would condemn the person and make him or her feel terrible. If you told him that you bought a new car, he would say that someone would rob you or that you would be fired from your job if your employer found out about it. If you wanted an advanced degree, he would say that you don't need to do anything else and to stay put where you are. If you wanted to start a business, he would give you every reason it would fail. Do you see where I'm going with this? This is the negativity my family has dealt with for years. One thing I noticed is that the few people, including myself, who have given him the figurative middle finger and moved forward with their lives despite his negativity have peace now and are doing well. The ones who are emotionally crippled and cannot stand up to my grandfather are now reinforcing that same cycle of poverty in their own homes now.

Isn't it funny how once you stand up to a bully (insert any person or generational curse) and take authority the table turns? The once big, bad wolf now knows it has no power over you and its attempts to keep you stagnant are null and void. This is why healing is so important. You do not have to subscribe to a life of lack, the status quo, and struggle just because you may have people in your life who have shortsighted vision. Tune out those negative voices and stay away from dream killers no matter who they are because their end goal is to keep you in the same position they are in.

My grandfather and I have had some serious fallouts and arguments due to his antics. However, once he realized that his antics didn't faze me and that I was going to live my life regardless of his commentary, the nonsense ceased. Now, he may try to step out of line, but he corrects himself now before I even have to because my line is permanently and deeply drawn in the sand.

CHAPTER 8:

Soul Tie Central

HOW CAN YOU IDENTIFY the generational curses in your life? Start by answering this question in written form: What are your hot buttons? Maybe you have an anger problem, a bad habit, or some other trigger. Ask yourself why you do certain things or act a certain way in specific situations. What are your set beliefs on life, love, and relationships? My generational issues showed in my relationships, and not just romantic relationships. Are you always being told you have an attitude or overreact too much or something along those lines? Why is that? These were questions I had to ask myself. Maybe yours aren't related to anger; perhaps you are easily offended, sensitive, or insecure, for example.

My generational issues created skewed views on people and relationships. I had an attitude of anti-submission. I believed I did not need to submit to anyone whether it was my husband or not. I felt that submitting to a man was something that I would never do. I could never answer why I felt that way until I peeled back the layers and took an introspective look at myself. I didn't want to submit because that equaled enduring the same type of abuse the women in my family suffered. I didn't want to be like them. However, my choices in men were still very poor.

Isn't it funny how we say that we will never do something or be a certain way but become the very thing that we hate? In my teenage years, I started dating, but from that point on I had a type of man toward whom I would always gravitate. This type of man was never abusive physically, which I believed was a good thing, but he sure was abusive mentally and emotionally. I liked the kind of man who was apparently weaker because I did not want someone who would ever raise his hand to me as I had witnessed so many times before. My goal was to spend my life with a man who was the opposite of the men in my family, but I didn't do a good job of that. My earlier romantic relationships made me feel so insecure. I am not blaming the men because I was immature as well. It is very telling that in my quest to avoid a certain type of guy I settled for a lesser evil and ended up with the disrespect that I despised from them anyway. This is an example of an unchecked generational curse. While running from the men who hurt me, I ran into the arms of men who were just as bad because I had not resolved those issues from the past. At the time I wasn't aware that I was caught up in a cycle or that there even *was* a cycle. Many are in the same boat. Having no idea why your behavior is the way it is or why you think the way that you do can be a curse in itself. I believe that truly getting to know yourself is important for your overall mental and emotional health. I was forced to get to know myself when my husband (my boyfriend at the time) and I had our son. I didn't realize how much of a complete and total mess I was until then. The mixture of post-partum depression and the sense that my identity was being stripped away by the loss of material things nearly sent me over the edge.

My husband and my closest uncle, Uncle Matt, helped bring things into perspective and get to the root of why my identity was so immersed in material things and why climbing the corporate ladder was more important to me than being a mother to my newborn baby. Looking back on that time, I realize now that I created such a façade about who I was that I didn't exist without those things. I was attracted to a different kind of guy from my uncles and grandfather. I liked to be in relationships where I wore the pants. I sought out guys who needed someone to mother them, stroke their egos constantly, and had no ambition. I thought I was dating the lesser of the two evils when I found a man who had at least one of those traits.

In my mind, I had to date this type of man in order to avoid being controlled or being treated the way the women in my life were. I equated the controlling and abusive behavior of the men in my family with strength. So, my simple-minded logic was that I did not want a strong man. In actuality, the men in my family weren't strong at all; they were weak. And the boys I dated were a different type of weak. At that point in my life, I wanted companionship, but I wouldn't have been able to handle a strong man anyway. I had no idea what defined a strong man. Mental and emotional abuse from the guys I dated was better than physical, verbal, and sexual abuse as far as I was concerned.

One relationship was the most toxic for me on a spiritual level, outside of the cheating lying, immaturity, and so forth. This particular relationship opened a spiritual door I didn't know existed. *Cue the soul tie.* I literally went through hell for about five years because of this soul tie, even after we had parted ways for good.

My sophomore year of college, I met this man named Lamont and we started dating. I was warned of his promiscuous reputation but I didn't care because I was so drawn to him. I felt that in due time I could change him…HA. Now everything was about sex and chemistry in this relationship before actual intercourse happened. People, perhaps especially women, tend to take that feeling of "fireworks" and misconstrue it for genuine feelings and a real future with someone.

One night, while we were intimate, we both climaxed simultaneously. I literally felt like I inhaled something as I took in that euphoric breath, as if I had sucked up an energy of some sort. As we walked back to our dormitories, things were strange and heavy between us, something I hadn't felt before. Nothing was wrong outwardly, but things felt different, and neither one of us could put our finger on what we were feeling.

I returned to my room, and we talked on the phone for a bit. I remember telling him that I felt "heavy" and probably needed to get some sleep. He said he felt the same way and that was the end of the phone call. I stayed awake for a few more minutes watching TV, but the heaviness I was feeling closed my eyes for me. That night, I felt like something was forcing my eyes closed. Again, I was chalking this up to being exhausted... or something. Moments later, I felt paralyzed and couldn't move. I yelled for my roommate, but my screams were silent— like I was trying to yell underwater. I saw a dark tail swipe across my face that was darker than the blackness of the room and then I heard something scurry underneath my covers. I was still paralyzed, still couldn't speak but I was able to witness everything as it happened, even as my physical body lay asleep.

My friends, this was a demonic attack.

I had never had one before until this moment, but oh boy, little did I know at the time that they were going to get worse over the next few years. All of this was given life because I slept with someone (and others) that I wasn't supposed to. We tend to feel, when we are young—not just chronological age, but mental age— that we can do as we please without any consequences. Being a free spirit isn't always free!

For the remainder of my time in college and afterward, my life was HELLISH spiritually. I was unable to sleep at night because I was so tormented by demons. I knew the moment I closed my eyes that the satanic forces would have their fun with me. The day after the first incident, strange things were happening. I went to the chapel on campus to speak with the life coaches. Their office was in a conference room where all of the musical instruments were stored against the wall. Out of nowhere, the drums fell as I was telling them what happened. That definitely freaked them out and they immediately confirmed that a negative energy was indeed present. Only certain people could see that my eyes were unnaturally red. I literally felt like darkness was hovering over me. I prayed and pleaded for whatever was wrong to go away, but it didn't. This was only the beginning of my torment. I was completely terrified, and the little faith I had was gone because in my mind I was being punished by God.

Desperate for some answers and guidance, I called my grandmother and told her in full detail what was happening. I asked her to pray with me and help me. My grandmother, who I saw as the pinnacle of faith, questioned what I had done to cause this and essentially blamed me, but couldn't tell me what I did. She said she wasn't familiar with what I was going through and instructed me to do some voodoo practices to rid myself of the demons. She suggested that I leave some pennies at my door to pay the spirits, place sulfur in my shoes, along with some other nonsense. I was desperate at the moment but not enough to entertain the demonic energy I was trying to get rid of. Yep, at that moment, I knew I was screwed. The woman who read her Bible every day, prayed and went to church religiously had no other advice to give me outside of resorting to voodoo practices. A Christian woman was telling me to do something that had nothing to do with her religion. From that moment forward, I knew I couldn't look to her for spiritual matters. See, this is why I am not a religious person. My grandmother's well-intentioned advice showed me that a religious person can do something out of habit or practice, but when it came time to apply what she had been practicing, she ran away toward something that was not aligned with her professed beliefs. What was the purpose of doing all that habitual practicing just to cower when the enemy really shows up? I thought to myself, we have been taught to run to God in our time of need, but her instructions were actually leading me away from Him. How ironic. Needless to say, I was disappointed.

Has anyone disappointed you when you needed him or her most? What happened? Grab your journal and write this question down for later.

The attacks increased and worsened, and still no one could tell me WHY they were happening or how to stop them.

One night I was arguing with Lamont after making a grocery run. It was quite our norm to be arguing about something, and most times it was something petty. I unloaded all of the items in my dorm and went to bed furious. Side note: Demons LOVE to find open doorways to come in and wreak havoc in your life. Discord, arguments, and negativity in general are perfect opportunities for them to come in and take over. It does not have to show up in your life as a literal demonic attack, but it will feel like a domino effect of negativity—one bad thing after the other—because the demons preyed on the negative energy you were feeding them. Going to bed angry was a win-win for the demons considering I was having nightly demonic attacks anyway.

Soon enough after going to bed angry, I felt paralyzed and could not utter a word. First, the handle of my door was spinning around and around, which was impossible for a door handle that could not be moved up but only be pushed down to open it. I felt like I was in the *Twilight Zone*: I was watching myself experience this, but was not able to do anything about it. Truly an out of body experience. A shadow then emerged from underneath the door. At first, the shadow was outside of the door like someone standing on the outside, but it was a face present instead of the shadow of a body. The shadow then entered the room. It moved swiftly to the wall that was to the right of my bed. I then felt myself being lifted from my bed by the neck. This demon then forcibly but slowly turned my head to face the wall so that I could see its silhouette. It was a three-headed demon that was grotesque and absolutely terrifying. I could only see the silhouette of this one, but it was still the most terrifying attack I have ever had because I was lifted out of bed. I was helpless in that moment. Once the demons finally freed me after terrorizing me and holding me by the neck in the air, all I could do was scream. I screamed and cried because the fear I was feeling was unfathomable. Unable to get help, confused about what to do, I just had to let these demonic encounters continue to happen. I have never felt so alone in my life. More than anything, I was trying to figure out what I had done to deserve such torment. Surely, I had pissed God off.

The attacks were out-of-body experiences. My physical body would be frozen but my spirit could see everything that is happening from like an aerial view. That is the clearest way that I can describe it. The attacks happened several times a week. It got to the point that I would sleep with a lamp on and a Bible underneath my pillow every single night because I was so scared. Once, I woke up and the Bible was adjacent from me, underneath my desk close to the wall. This was absolutely impossible for me to do in my sleep because I would have to get up, throw it low and in a curve, and it would have had to miss the chair. Again, super impossible. This is just one example of how the demons would do other things to make their presence known aside from actual attacks. I dreaded nightfall because I knew I would have unwanted visitors.

Another thing I have learned is that demonic spirits prey on your weaknesses to attack. I mentioned before that after arguing with my ex Lamont, the demons saw that negative energy as a doorway to attack. An attack does not have to be as dramatic as the ones I am describing; they can also affect everyday aspects of your life. If you are fearful, insecure, angry, or pompous, the enemy will play on that weakness, thus opening a door through which he can send his troubles to you. You will find your relationships with others always in shambles; you will fail to have peace in your life; and be robbed of joy. Because of all this upheaval, you are not checking your vulnerabilities and uprooting them through healing and acknowledgement that you have some issues to work on.

My grandfather is an example of this. He is in his 80s and he is still a very callous and ornery man. Any little thing can set him off, and the enemy (Satan) absolutely loves that he can use my grandfather as a host to do his dirty work. This man is ALWAYS angry about something. There is never a moment of peace with him. Unfortunately, he has allowed this energy to engulf him completely, so to my grandfather, oozing negativity is normal. Satan knows he is a fearful person and he plays on my grandfather's fears. My grandfather's fears then turn to anger, which turns to unstable relationships and behavior.

What are your weaknesses? Have you checked them? Don't allow yourself to be used by the enemy!

I have been with my husband for five years now, and I have had nothing but peace as far spiritual attacks go. The infrequent attacks I have now are always warnings for someone else. There is so much more to abstaining until marriage than meets the eye. That's not to say you won't have problems by waiting, but I truly believe if you have married the one who is meant for you, you can avoid a lot craziness like demonic attacks from soul ties if you make the decision to wait until you are married to make love.

I have two children. After growing up with deceptive and secretive adults, I am determined to stick to my keep-it-real initiative with my son and daughter. When my son asks questions, instead of brushing him off, I tell him the truth in the most age-appropriate manner. I am convinced that constantly hiding things from your children does not help them at all. It causes them to jump to their own conclusions, and ultimately leads to confusion. I notice that when I give him a straightforward and honest answer, he has no further questions afterward. When it comes to life, sex, goals, and dreams, I plan to be completely transparent with them and allow them to create their own paths in the hopes that they won't make the same mistakes that I did. During my spiritual confusion with soul ties, no one was able to help me to until years later. I wish someone would have been able to know exactly the direction to steer me instead of looking at me like I was crazy every time I sought help. My children will not be left out in the dark about anything if I can help it.

Speaking of children, in the midst of all of the spiritual turmoil I was experiencing in 2006 with Lamont, two years later, during my senior year of college, I became pregnant. This was a terrible experience because I continued to deal with someone who I KNEW was not good for me, and I had the audacity to get pregnant by him. My senior year was quite rough, not academically but personally. I was depressed, stressed out, and alone because I had damaged the relationships of those close to me due to my attitude. I felt like I needed Lamont despite him being toxic, his constant cheating, lack of ambition, and other negative factors. He was what I clung to because I didn't love myself enough to walk away.

With all of the demonic attacks happening and knowing that Lamont would not be present in the life of the baby I was carrying I decided to have an abortion. What sent me over the edge was finding out for the millionth time that he was cheating. I couldn't take it anymore, I completely blacked out, destroyed his dormitory room, and threatened to kill the baby on sight and possibly hurt myself. Some of the drama came from my hormones raging in that moment. The only thing that stopped me from possibly cutting his throat was him calling my mother. She talked me out of continuing to make a complete fool of myself. I decided right then that I was not going through with the pregnancy. I fled to Charlotte and had the procedure done. Now overall, I believe that women have the right to make whatever decisions they need to regarding their bodies. I do not believe that this should be used irresponsibly as if it is a form of birth control. With that said, I remember very clearly after having the procedure feeling a heavy weight lifted off of my chest. Like a spiritual release happened in that moment. It was strange to me because I expected to feel terrible afterward. Instead, I felt free spiritually, at peace, and relieved. I must stress that in no way am I trying to come off as insensitive in any way, but this is exactly how my experience happened and this was my reaction to it. However, I do know people who have had abortions and still struggle with the guilt of having had them. Everyone responds differently to things, which is to be expected. I truly believe that I saved myself and that child the heartache, stress, and anguish of being without a father and continuing the cycle of generational curses.

CHAPTER 9:

Types of Soul Ties

SOUL TIES AND GENERATIONAL CURSES are like siblings—not identical, but closely related. Soul ties can take different forms. They do not always take the form that mine did via literal demonic attacks. Sometimes soul ties can be formed when you stay with someone knowing they are only making withdrawals from your life but continue to stay with them because they are comfortable. My cousin and I refer to these as dirty blankets. To make it more formal I will call these self-induced soul ties. The dirty blanket is comfy, we have always had them, but we know full well they should've have been discarded a long time ago. Outside of these blankets being filthy, they are also useless because they have holes in them. So now we are keeping them around solely for familiarity and because they can't realistically provide us comfort anymore.

We can all become stuck on the illusion that they are nice and fluffy blankets because that is how they once appeared to us. In reality, they have always been dirty blankets. These blankets can be relationships where you are with someone, you fall in love with the person's representative or what you have created the person to be in your mind, and because of the illusion you refuse to let go of, you stay in a draining and pointless relationship. You reject all logic in the name of—you guessed it—POTENTIAL. Like Brandy said in one of her songs, "almost doesn't count." Nearly every relationship I had prior to my husband was based on potential.

Luckily, I have learned my lesson, and you can, too. It is best to just accept someone for who he is from the beginning. Stop imagining that person to be someone else in order to be the perfect mate for you. Either accept him for the ambitionless bum that he is or keep it moving. Beware that staying in a relationship where you continue to hope and wish or think someone will change will be more of a headache for you than that person because he will never change not because of you anyway.

Did that hurt? Good! You are one step closer to getting out of your current pointless situationship. Do not continue to be a victim of a self -induced soul tie. Snap out of la-la land and break free. Stick with me and I will walk you through how to snap out of it, but you have to be *ready* to do so.

Another type of soul tie is a situational soul tie. So, let's say that you were hard-headed and decided to stay with your dirty blanket against that gut instinct—also known as your better judgement. You and dirty blanket end up having a child together, so now you feel even more stuck with this person. You have now tied yourself to someone because you both have created a life together. Now you feel obligated to make it work for the sake of the child. There is nothing wrong with that commitment initially, but let's be honest. If your dirty blanket has remained the same the entire relationship with *you,* what in the world will having a child do to make your dirty blanket change? Bringing a baby into the situation will only create more disappointment and stress for you. I am sure you thought that maybe if the sweet baby came along that it would suddenly awaken something in the person to morph into the ideal mate you have always dreamed of. You couldn't be more wrong. Having a child with someone you know you should've have left alone the moment you met him will only add to the chaos. This person who will not change under any circumstances; but convinces you that he will has caused you to produce a child with him. Now I call this situational because you aren't truly stuck with this person. It is the situation that is causing the tie that may still be present. However, I am a firm believer that nothing is unfixable. You can still sever the tie even though you have a child with this person or whatever the "situation" may be, it is up to you to sever the tie and move forward. Come to think of it, a self-induced soul tie and a situational one can be interchangeable, but the situational tie is a factor outside of the two parties contributing the tie. In this case, the tie is a baby.

Speaking of kids, it is important that you are careful not to reproduce with someone you know has issues. If you know for a fact that the person is not good for you, you must face the fact that he would definitely not be good for a kid. As the late Maya Angelou said, "when someone shows you who they are, believe them the first time." This is where generational curses and soul ties become intertwined. You are with someone not worth a dime and he makes your life hell. That is a soul tie. If you are with someone who isn't worth a crap and then you have a baby together, you are now making the baby susceptible to a generational curse. Why? Because now the unresolved hurt and pain that you have endured from this toxic relationship can unintentionally be placed on the child. For example, there are some women and men who constantly tell their children that they are just like the other parent in a negative way. "You are going to be sorry just like your dad" or "all men are worthless like your dad" are examples of attaching your hurt to a child. Additionally, the wayward parent also contributes to the destruction of the child and the generational cycle continues.

So, let me tell you a story about a guy, a woman, and a horrible soul tie that affected everyone around them. He met an older woman when he was in his late teens. She was possibly in her mid-20s. She not only already had a small child, but she was also married. Yeah, so things already started off way wrong in this relationship. In his late teens, I am sure this guy was not thinking of the consequences of dealing with a married woman, but he would soon find out what they were. When you are dating or just having fun, you must consider the nature of a person before getting serious with him or her. This young man didn't consider the fact that a woman who is willing to cheat on her spouse with him would also do the same to him. No, you are not special so please cut the shenanigans and stop making excuses saying your situation is different.

Anyway, the young man began a relationship with this married woman, who then gave her child to her husband because "she can't take care of him." Translation: she wanted to be free to do what she pleased without being tied down with the responsibilities of being a parent. That move on her part should have been another huge red flag for the young man. So, not only was this person cheating on her husband with the young man, but she then gives her child up without flinching so she could go party and do whatever else.

Would this end well?

So, the relationship continued. They were having fun: she is exposing him to the exciting parts of life—drugs, threesomes, and other activities—and the young man thought everything was great. The woman became pregnant and she rushed him to get married a couple of months prior to giving birth. Apparently, despite everything she had done up to that point, her "morals" kicked in and she couldn't stand the thought of bringing a child into the world out of wedlock.

Hmmm, is that her only concern?

So, they had a shotgun wedding, and soon after the kid was born. The guy in this scenario grew up immediately and matured once the child was born. He now realized he could no longer live the carefree life he had once enjoyed. (You know, because having a kid requires responsibility and accountability.) However, the woman didn't get that memo. Now remember she gave custody of her eldest child to her ex-husband because she didn't want the responsibility, so what would change now that she had given birth to a second child? You guessed it, nothing! The deadbeat title isn't just for dads; moms can be deadbeats, too.

So, the guy realized that this woman he married and had a child with had no intention of changing. By now, her mental health issues were shining through like never before; she continued to drink and do drugs heavily; she spent the money of the household on everything but the bills; abandoned the child emotionally; and completely drove this man's life into a black hole. After several years of dealing with this and coming to the conclusion that she was incapable of caring about anyone but herself (shocker) the guy filed for divorce and moved on with his life. Once the divorce was finalized, he was granted primary custody of the child.

Now, you REALLY have to be a deficient mother for the courts to grant custody to the father. Typically, (although not always best) custody is automatically given to the mom. Since he was given custody of the child, of course what was next was child support. His now ex-wife was not at all happy about being forced to pay child support because she felt that she shouldn't have to contribute financially to the child's wellbeing solely because she was the mother.

Makes a lot of sense, huh? Well, maybe not so much.

This guy went through hell in an effort to try to protect the child from her mother's issues—generational curses: drug and alcohol abuse, mental health issues, or lack of accountability—and provide her with as normal as a life as possible. He spent thousands of dollars on legal fees, counseling for his daughter, and psychiatric visits because the child was later diagnosed with a mental impairment due to their behavioral problems. This man fought an uphill battle trying to co-parent with a woman who didn't care about the child but who wanted to maintain control.

I forgot to mention an important point though. The moment he filed for divorce, the woman began saying that the child was not his and that he shouldn't try to get custody, (So, you mean to tell me this woman made this man marry her on the strength of her being pregnant, yet, the entire time she knew that she wasn't pregnant by him?) She started saying the child wasn't his continuously, especially every time they went to court. The guy could not bring himself to believe that he had been duped in the worst possible way, so he didn't get a DNA test when she brought it up initially. He thought she was saying it out of bitterness and not truth.

The guy finally mustered up the courage to get a DNA test due to the extremely stressful nature of the situation. To make matters worse, the child rejected him although she lived with this man, who was the only father she had ever known. The DNA test results came, and... Voila! There was a 0% chance that the young man could be this child's father. Can you imagine the pain, shock, and anguish this man felt when he got those results? Everything he had done had been for the sake of the child. All the hell he had endured was all for the kid. This man had reacted in a normal way; a parent is supposed to do what he or she has to do for his or her child, no matter what.

Now after DNA results were revealed, things got even stickier for this man. The mother was so hellbent on making the guy's life miserable that she began to manipulate the child emotionally and mentally more than she ever had. As a result, the child became extremely difficult to raise under the man's roof, but he couldn't figure out why. Unbeknownst to the young man, the girl's mother began telling the child that the man was not her real father, and that she didn't have to listen to him or respect him. Of course, such underhandedness is a recipe for disaster in the custodial parent's household. What is the most heartbreaking part of this is that the mother could not have cared less about how all of this would damage the child later on in her life. The truth will always come to light, and unfortunately one day she will find out about all of the lies her mother told that led up to this point. This is another example of how unchecked soul ties and generational curses beget more of the same.

Fast forward a few years. After extensive counseling and more legal actions, the man decided that it was best to terminate his parental rights to a child he had raised since birth and part ways with that child. For the sake of his own sanity, he allowed the child to be where she wanted to be, which was with her mom despite how toxic and detrimental she was to her. Ouch!

Do you see how nasty generational curses and soul ties can get? This story involved a damaged woman and a naïve guy. The guy didn't know all of the baggage the woman was carrying, was easily manipulated since he was young and immature and from that seemingly simple involvement, a situation from hell was born. This woman clearly had some unhealed hurts and generational curses that she had inherited that had gone unchecked. Otherwise, she would have been incapable of hurting people and sucking them into such toxicity. The fact that she did it to her own children speaks volumes. She was an octopus of unchecked generational curses and anyone within her reach was sure to be sucked into it.

You cannot be with—let alone procreate with— someone like that. Your life will go downhill immediately and very quickly. In this story, the man was totally oblivious to the forces he was dealing with and fell for the woman's trickery under the guise of excitement with someone, and paid for it dearly. He wasted many years of his life with someone he was never meant to be with, and, in the process, lost a child who, although not his biological daughter, he was committed to rearing. Now that child is dealing with generational curses in her own life and isn't even aware that her mom is so manipulative and conniving. Unfortunately, as she chases her mother looking for her to love them, she will continue to be met with hurt and disappointment as she battles against the generational curses laid before her and the ones she is dealing with as an individual now.

Again, unchecked generational curses don't just affect *you*; they affect whomever you date, your children, and the quality of your life after that person. It is a true snowball of chaos if you choose not to break free once the red flags start waving. Additionally, it is always good to ask God for wisdom, discernment, and extreme sensitivity to Him so you can easily back away from situations before they get completely out of hand. That's not to say that things will be perfect because we are imperfect and will make mistakes. Actually, we learn from a lot of our mistakes and they help us become better people. I share this so hopefully you avoid pitfalls and unnecessary drama. I know we all have to go through things and learn lessons for ourselves, but you don't always have to let your hard head make a soft behind. Take a detour and save yourself some time.

CHAPTER 10:

Unintentionally Creating Your Own Stains

WE HAVE ALL HEARD SOMEONE say or have said that we would never do something or be like someone. Then as time passed, we became that very thing or person we didn't like. How does this happen? It is simple and also complicated. When you haven't dealt with old wounds from your past whether you were bullied, raped, or saw a family member struggle with addiction, and so forth, instead of uprooting that hurt and healing, you probably ran toward it. (You are not alone.) Your efforts are futile when your focus is on "I'll show them" or "I will never be that kind of parent" or other resolutions like that. You completely miss your intended mark because your focus is not directed correctly. You create these false realities and end up not truly living for yourself or in your complete truth because you have allowed fear to drive you. (You are not alone in this, either.) Sometimes it can temporarily work in your favor, but eventually you will end up miserable and spinning your wheels.

Fear is never a good motivator. Let's exchange fear with acceptance. I know you are thinking, *why in the world should I accept what has happened to me?* Well, once you accept it, you will no longer run away from it, which also means you won't run right back to it. Acceptance can take many different forms. It helps you to own what has taken place in your life, not allow it to define you, and release its control over you. Acceptance does not mean allowing others to run over and manipulate you, nor does it mean wallowing in your sorrows. Acceptance means forgiving the person or yourself. Any harbored unforgiveness does not hurt the person who hurt you; it only hurts you, every time. If you have been wronged in any way or watched those closest to you do others wrong, don't hate them and allow your hatred to distort your view of life and people. Also, if you are the person who has now become the abuser, manipulator, alcoholic, or whatever the issue is, I urge you to seek the root of this behavior. When did your life take a turning point? Dig deep and really think about your earliest memory of when your life changed. If there was an emotional scale, how much would your baggage weigh? Release the baggage! No one has to stay the same, and no one has to be held captive to his or her mistakes. The change starts with you and a decision. You already know that not making this life change will hold you back because you are reading this book in search of a starting point.

Let me give a simple example of how our experiences can morph into another link in the generational chain from which we are trying to escape. My son was having Grandparents Day at his school and my mother was able to attend. While in his classroom, she started looking at me and pointing to another little black boy, aggressively mouthing "watch him, watch him." I was mortified and embarrassed and told her to stop pointing at this child, especially when I had seen that he had done nothing to cause her to do this. We got in the car and I asked her why was she singling this child out. She said, "because he is the biggest child in his class and those are the types to push and shove." At this point I was so annoyed with my mom and shocked by her behavior. I reminded her that this was a stereotype that our young black males have to deal with constantly, even when they have done absolutely nothing wrong. She looked at this four-year-old baby who was minding his business and said that he was a problem. Of course, I let my mom know that she was perpetuating the same stereotypes and fears that have been passed down (another example of a generational curse) about blacks and she is black herself. Oy vey.

Anyway, as we returned to my home and my mother told me that she was ashamed of her behavior and didn't realize that she was pointing at the boy or singling him out. On the ride home, she said that she was so ashamed that she wondered why she would behave that way towards an innocent toddler. She disclosed that she was bullied as a child because she was the youngest and smallest of her classmates. Now that she has a grandson who is in school, she realized that she was projecting her experiences of being bullied on to him. Though her actions were unintentional, because in that moment she felt she was being protective of my son, she had, in reality, become the bully she didn't like growing up.

See that?

Unresolved hurts and issues do manifest themselves later in life. You will become what you despise if you don't uproot your mess. Now, I must say I am proud of my mom and that she has come a long way. If this had happened years ago, and I had called her out about her behavior, she would've panicked and swept the problem under the rug. However, she took a moment to figure out why she was acting the way she was, where it came from, and initiated a dialogue about it. In that moment, I gained a greater understanding of my mom and our relationship grew. A precious healing took place within her and between us. She owned that she had been bullied as a child, that it had a negative effect on her, and that she had become a bully without realizing. Better still, she corrected herself and resolved the hurt. I bet she won't do something like that again. Once you are aware of what you are doing, you can determine its origin, and uproot it. You will then be free.

Do not let your unresolved hurts lead you on a path of destruction. To be a willing participant in chaos is asinine. However, there are times when you don't even realize and recognize that your actions are a detriment to yourself and others, or at least you don't want to admit it. I honestly believe you are more susceptible to soul ties when you haven't acknowledged and healed from your generational curse. You are walking around damaged, and damaged people are ultimately what you will attract in your relationships (not just romantic ones).

I believe with all of my heart that 99% of personality flaws come from unresolved hurt and pain from our past. If we don't dig deep and get to the origin of our behaviors, we will continue the vicious cycle of projecting our issues onto others, passing the negativity to our children, and robbing ourselves of peace.

I know that you have met someone who is always causing discord in his or her relationships. Whether it was a personal or professional relationship, this troubled person is always in the middle, stirring up drama and refusing to acknowledge that he or she is the problem. These energy vampires need healing. When people used to upset me constantly and create issues that otherwise wouldn't have been there, I would question myself and try to figure out what was wrong with me. It took me a long time to figure out that these people weren't really upset with me. Rather, they are still dealing with stuff from their pasts and they don't even realize it.

The way such a person is treating you badly is the result of the way someone or a group of people treated them. So instead of living healthy, peaceful lives, they are walking wounds, spewing their pus on everyone instead of treating the infection properly and healing.

A friend of mine had a nightmare client who was obnoxious, rude, and condescending. Now I know you may be thinking, "it's work; you have to deal with difficult people all the time, so get over it." This is true in most cases, but this lady was a special case. Her demands and attitude became so ridiculous that even my friend's boss acknowledged that they will not take on that client again because she was causing unnecessary stress on all his employees. Yeah, it was that bad.

Anyway, as I talked to my friend about this client, it hit me that it was not my friend's company that was the problem. I was certain that the client's home life was a wreck, which was why she was on a mission to make everyone else's life hell. It was as if this client was saying, "I'm going to give what I'm getting at home or what I would like to give so that I can feel better about my internal mess." That is how damaged people work and think.

I challenge you to look a little deeper when you are dealing with people like my friend's client. Instead of allowing them to spew their pus on you (I chose this graphic imagery intentionally; think about how people like this poison your life.), use it as an opportunity to pray for the person's healing. If at all possible, maybe you can be a light in that person's life by showing him or her that you are unaffected by his or her behavior and continue to go about your business without any interference from the person.

Now, for some people, especially in personal relationships, the boundary has to be drawn and distance has to be made. I don't feel that people should subject themselves to chaos just because someone else wants to live like that. In all of my toxic relationships with family members or friends, once I drew the line and made it clear what I would not accept, they no longer crossed the line with me. If they did, they would lose access to me completely. My peace is important to me, and yours should be to you, too.

You can also think of toxic professional relationships as indirect generational curses. People who cause these toxic relationships are emotional disasters and are trying to pass on that generational link to others by being a contemptible person. So, generational stuff not only affects your family and those after you, but it can taint every area of your life. Could you be the cause of a toxic professional relationship? Please check yourself to ensure that you are not the problem. A mission to be mean is hurting you the most, but also chipping away at others' peace of mind.

The actions of hurt people who hurt others can also place a magnifying glass on your own unresolved stuff. How? The way you handle a hurt person's treatment can sometimes let you know if there are things you can do to heal in your own life. For example, this toxic person may trigger your anxiety, insecurities, self-doubt, and other issues. We already know this hurt individual has issues and also that sometimes it truly is that person, and not us. However, there are times when we have to ask ourselves why we respond to them or are triggered by them. Why do you have anxiety and insecurities anyway? When did those things start to form in your life? Why is what this person doing taking you to that place? Keep in mind that you can also attract certain energies by our own weaknesses. I know this is an extremely tangled web with so many different layers. I just need you to see that we are very complex beings who are interconnected and the way we are has an explanation.

CHAPTER 11:

Daddy Issues

A FUNNY THING HAPPENED BEFORE I wrote this section. I was never going to talk about my dad in this book...at all. My omission of him was deliberate. I even mentioned him for a half a second and made sure to tell you that I wouldn't be going into details about him. My attitude toward mentioning him should've let me know that I still had some healing to do when it comes to my father. I thought those feelings were gone and uprooted. I guess not. Although this section is in the middle of the book, this is the last thing I wrote....I had to add this in. This is an important piece to my life and healing. It touches on generational curses, soul ties (even if it isn't yours directly) and unintentionally making your own link in the chain of generational curses.

My mother met my father while she was in college. She told me that her inexperience in dating in addition to not knowing how to identify a "good" man based on her family history is what caused her to be attracted to my dad. My dad was very intelligent and a little eccentric in his thinking.

Shortly after they began dating, my mother became pregnant with the queen herself...me. All was well between them while they were dating. Isn't that always the case, though? When we are dating people, we tend to only date their representatives. Heck, we are representatives as well. It's not until the person gets comfortable with us, hard times happen, and other factors that we begin to learn the other person's true colors.

My dad completely flipped once my mom became pregnant and basically abandoned her. Suddenly she became an inconvenience to him. The party was officially over. My grandparents forced them to have a shotgun wedding months into her pregnancy. I do not understand that. In my opinion, just because you are pregnant by someone shouldn't mean you should be pressured into marriage. A forced marriage seems to make situations worse than they are and adds additional stuff to sort through emotionally and otherwise. One major life event at a time please.

When they went to retrieve the marriage license, my mother also found out that my dad had been married before. This was one of million red flags that were waving for my mom. She proceeded to marry him anyway. Shortly after I turned two, my brother was born. My mom and dad were only married two years at this point but their marriage was about to end. My mom finally left my dad after he backslapped her as she was holding my brother, who was barely a month old.

I remember visiting with my dad when I was a child and craving his attention. My mom said I would always ask about him. When I was with him I was in an adult environment—lots of drinking, smoking, and sexual crap going on for me to see. My dad was so negligent that once when I was a toddler and in his care, I somehow got out of the house and was roaming the streets. Relatives had to come search for me because doing drugs and women was more important to him than watching his baby girl.

Eventually, my dad fell off the face of the earth. I didn't really think about him again until I was 16 years old and realized there was still a gaping hole in my heart. I wanted my dad and to have that relationship with him despite his absence. I decided to write him a letter with a ton of questions. I was looking to him to affirm me in spite of his faults. Cue the start of my uncontrollable neediness and insecurity. My dad did write me back, but he answered none of my questions, didn't affirm me, and only asked about my brother. Insert gut punch. I made a lot of efforts to connect with him, and my mom even helped me to do so, although she told me not to get my hopes up.

He came to my high school graduation. My birthday was the next day. I waited for him to call me and wish me a happy 18th birthday, even though he had never given me anything for my birthday before. I grew tired of waiting and called him. I asked him if he knew what day it was, especially since I had seen him the day before. He didn't even know when my birthday was, and instead of apologizing, he countered by asking me when I had ever called him for Father's Day. What a complete and total jerk! Another gut punch.

The good that has come from holiday visits, which I had to initiate with him, and invitations to life events is that I have permanently connected with his side of the family. I consider myself to be close to my dad's side of the family and I love them so much because they embraced me even though he never has, even to this day. They have been a huge part of my healing, and I am forever grateful for their openness and honesty. They have never made me feel like his absence or abandonment was my fault. They have stood in the gap.

For a lot of my life, I was a wandering little girl in search of her father, in search of love, wanting to feel wanted, worthy, and complete. My last attempt to contact my father was when I pregnant with my son. Now by that point, my dad's mental illness was very obvious, but everything he did still mattered to me. I called him to announce my pregnancy of his first grandchild and his response was "this is all you called to tell me?"

Final gut punch.

So, this horrible reaction, coupled with all of the crap I endured from him as a child, was a nice recipe for an insecure, hurting adult with low self-esteem and too much pride and anger.

The reason I felt a huge push to write about my dad is because my husband and I got into an argument. For the past three years, I have been begging my husband to be more romantic, affirm me verbally, and provide me with all things mushy. He is a laid back guy and an introvert so he isn't that type of person. However, when he did step outside of himself and give me what I believed I needed, I still felt that it wasn't enough. I still needed more. That more that I was convinced I needed wasn't something that he could give, though. The more that I was looking for had to come from within me. I wanted my husband to patch up hurts that existed long before he came on the scene, wounds so deep that the love he had for me couldn't stitch it together.

I realized that instead of demanding that my husband fill the voids in my life, I had to dig within and fill them myself. Although he has brought me much joy and helped me through so much, there are still things that I have to take care of on my own. It's unfair to hold someone hostage emotionally because you still have unresolved stuff to work out within yourself. This is why relationships cannot be 50/50. You both need to be whole or at least working toward becoming whole, otherwise you will keep taking from one another to get to 100%. If you are just about whole—no one is perfect—before getting into the relationship, then the give and take is more balanced and not as detrimental to the other person as it could be when one or both have unresolved or undiscovered hurts.

I had to make a decision to sever the generational curse of fatherlessness. Every day I affirm myself and speak good things to myself to rid myself of the negative thoughts I have had due to my dad's absence from my life. Instead of looking to someone else to tell me my worth, I look within for it. Don't get me wrong though; validation from others is like a wonderful cherry on top of hard-earned self-esteem. However, we have to be assured already on our own, so no matter what happens, we are left intact.

For me, this section is the most important, and I even shed tears while writing because I refuse to let my dad and his absence continue to leave me empty. That emptiness was not only affecting the way I viewed myself, but also how I viewed my husband and marriage. Writing this section enabled me to give you advice that I strive to follow: stop believing the lies you have been telling yourself and start telling yourself the truth.

You are beautiful, you are worthy, you are amazing, you are strong, you are intelligent, you are capable. You can do this!!!

IDENTIFYING CURSES AND TIES RECAP

Grab Your Journals!

I have taken you through many direct and indirect examples of generational curses and soul ties from my life and the people in it. With these examples, your wheels should be turning with key events that have taken place in your life. Remember, everything counts. No event is too small to be considered a significant part of your life!

1. Are you suffering because of the actions of someone before you? What did this person or these persons do? Be specific.
2. List the attitudes, behaviors, or habits that you inherited because of the hurt you endured from someone else? Have you created one or more because of someone else? List them, too.
3. Are there any relatives of yours (even if it is you) that remind you of the people I mentioned in the chapter? If so, discuss the similarities and describe the behaviors of the people in your life.
4. List the specific generational curses and soul ties that are impacting you.

SPOT REMOVAL

Once you start to notice the stains on the hand-me-downs, sometimes you are likely to want to see if you can treat the stains to get the garment as close to new as possible. Most people do the same once they realize they have issues in their lives by treating them to make the stains less noticeable, or at least we think.

CHAPTER 12:

A Call to Action

S O FAR, WE HAVE DEFINED generational curses and soul ties, taken an inside look at the ones I have personally seen and experienced, and figured out how to identify them. Now we must figure out how to move forward from all the damage that has been done. We have gone through several examples of generational curses and soul ties. It is only right that we dig into success stories of how I have overcome them in addition to celebrating the victories of others who have healed as well. Healing is an ongoing process, so although those I mentioned and I have taken our issues up by their roots, we still have to do maintenance work and keep weeds from sprouting up.

After unknowingly dealing with the stains of recurring issues in my family and becoming a product of them, the burdens of the past finally became too heavy for me to wear. Things really hit a turning point when I became a mother. Did I want this attitude and way of thinking to be passed on to my children? Giving birth to my son showed me how severely damaged I was. Four years ago, I finally started my process of unlearning everything I had been taught and relearning spiritually, mentally, and emotionally. My point is not to blame anyone because we all have our faults, but hopefully the events of my life will help you peel back the layers of your own life so that you can sever the ties that have you bound. Ask yourself why you react this way to certain things, why are certain issues hot buttons for you, and where did your views on life begin. Take an introspective look at yourself today and begin your healing process to uproot what is holding you hostage. I truly hope that the personal experiences that I have shared with you give you courage. As I write this, I, too, am doing maintenance work on my own healing.

In 2012, after giving birth to my son, I was absolutely miserable. I was having a quarter life crisis—seriously. I had always been this very independent woman who felt that I didn't need a man for any reason based on what I witnessed growing up. I met my husband in 2011, and things escalated quickly between us before too long, my son arrived. I was working in the mental health field and was working my way up to receive my license in professional counseling. I switched gears academically once I was far enough along in my pregnancy. I realized that mental health wasn't my calling as I once thought that it was. I wanted to help people, but not within the red tape of the mental health system. There were so many times I wanted to help people or offer advice, but I couldn't because of procedure, protocol, and ethics. Additionally, I knew, once I started my first year in my master's program for professional counseling, that I wouldn't continue because taking on the burdens of others would have burned me out.

I am a pretty emotional person as it is and I just couldn't see myself going forward. Have you ever thought that you have found your calling but actually you were chasing after something for the wrong reasons? *Come on; raise your hand. * My attraction to psychology was because of my screwed-up family. There. I said it. I was always curious about why people were the way they were and what drove them to do certain things. My family is the reason for that curiosity. Before I went to college, I was never honest with myself about why I chose my major, but now I can be honest and say that subconsciously I was looking to fill a void in my life. I wanted to heal others when I needed healing myself.

So back to my quarter life crisis. When I was in the middle of my pregnancy with my son, I was working at a psychiatric hospital in addition to being a paraprofessional for families and disadvantaged youth. Working those types of jobs became extremely stressful for me, and were not conducive to a healthy pregnancy. So, I left my jobs and my future husband offered to let me stay with him. At first I was okay with it, but then my attitude really started to change. I began to feel worthless because I wasn't contributing to the household. I did not like depending on a man to take care of me. Throughout the entire pregnancy and after my son was born, I griped about how I should be contributing and how worthless I was...blah blah blah. It nearly killed me to have a man take care of me. A part of me felt like this was something that he could hold over my head and in the blink of an eye my baby and I could be out on the street.

Now, my husband is the nicest guy I have ever met. He is so kind and would never do anything to hurt anyone, honestly. My insecurities came from watching the women in my family be taken care of by men who were supposed to love them only to be slapped in the face later for it—literally and figuratively.

At that time, I felt that I had made a horrible mistake by allowing myself to become pregnant because now I was at the mercy of a man. I couldn't recognize that I actually had a sincere and good man because of the examples of men I had had in my life. My link to the chain of the generational curses was showing itself. There couldn't possibly be a man who existed who would take care of a woman and his child genuinely without anything in return or feeling like he owned the woman. I couldn't love my husband properly at the time because I didn't know how; I didn't know what real love or a healthy relationship looked like. I only knew immaturity, manipulation, abuse, and all things negative. I just knew that if I let my guard down and let this man love me that he would have something to hang over my head and have an excuse to try to control me. None of this was true about him; it was all in my head and direct result of my internal battle with generational curses.

One day soon after our son was born, I was having one of my post-partum breakdowns about feeling useless and wanting to be the strong woman I felt I needed to be to avoid mistreatment. My husband looked at me and said "I don't know who you are or what has happened but I want my Debbie back." I don't know why, but when he said that I realized I had some serious issues. The look of desperation on his face was pitiful. I had to stop and ask myself what in the world I was doing to make a grown man desperate for me to get it together. I realized I was suffering from a few things: post-partum depression, generational curses, and a prideful attitude that had come from me creating a defense mechanism to combat the generational issues.

Now, along with my husband calling me out, I was still lost and confused about who I was, what was wrong, and what I needed to do to fix myself. I have three uncles I can call on and talk to about absolutely anything. They are wonderful people inside and out. One in particular, Uncle Matt, has been like a father to me my whole life and has guided me in every way. He is my go-to for advice and a sounding board.

In 2005, soon after I graduated from high school, my grandfather and I had an argument prior to me leaving for college. I called my uncle to vent, and he asked, "why are you so angry?" After a four-hour conversation, I realized that I had anger towards my grandfather from watching what he had done to my mother and grandmother when I was a child. It took peeling back some serious layers in that phone conversation for me to figure out what was truly the root of my attitude. This conversation with my uncle started my spot removal process. At the time, I had memories that were so suppressed I didn't realize they had helped me become an angry, combative person towards certain relatives. I didn't know why until then. Sometimes we have so much baggage and unhealed hurts that it gets to a point that we don't actively realize why we are even behaving in the way that we are; it becomes a part of us.

Fast forward to 2012 and I am calling my Uncle Matt again. This time to figure out why I was so unhappy although I was with a great guy and had a sweet newborn to care for. So, over a 7 year span I had finally gotten to the root of why I was doing the things I was doing. As I mentioned in an earlier section, I started to use material things to patch up my past instead of dealing with the hurt directly. Solange's song, Cranes in the Sky, is a perfect example of what happens when we are doing everything but dealing with the hurt in our lives directly to mask the pain or at least that is my interpretation. Now I was finally ready to face the pain head on. Cue ripping the bandage off of the hairiest arm possible.

CHAPTER 13:

It's Never Too Late to Heal

I HAVE DISCUSSED MY MOTHER and the turmoil that she has endured at length. However, there is a happy ending to her story or should I say a happy beginning. My mom and I have always had a relationship where I felt comfortable voicing my concerns to her. I was always desperately looking for her to reciprocate or meet me halfway. The blockage was always her unhealed heart. Our emotional relationship was strained because she didn't know how to emotionally connect with me. That then spilled over into her relationship with my son, her first grandchild. I would tell her since you couldn't be there for my brother and me, you should use your grandchild as a fresh start emotionally.

So, a few years go by and my child is now a toddler. My mother would only come around if I begged, pleaded, and accommodated her to do so. It was draining because no matter how much advanced notice I gave her, she would make every excuse in the world as to why she couldn't spend time with her grandchild. Her past and the fear it generated in her paralyzed her. Her fear was beginning to rob her of a life with her grandchild.

Things came to head when my husband and I were expecting our second child. In the 20th week of my pregnancy, I suddenly went into premature labor resulting in the loss of our daughter. My husband and I were so broken from this loss that it almost tore us apart. We were so wrecked. Now, this was my mother's second grandchild. I did not hear from her for an entire week—no visit to the hospital, no offer to take care of my son, no call, no encouragement. My mom went MIA the moment she found out. When she finally did call, I had a massive meltdown and went off on her. I couldn't believe that she could be absent in what was probably the most traumatic time of my life. However, that meltdown and loss was the best thing that could've ever happened to our relationship.

I forced my mother to explain why she had been absent at a time when I needed her most. I sobbed as I begged her to stop punishing me for the sins of my grandmother. She understood my meaning immediately: "just because *your* mother wasn't there for you when you needed her most, don't hurt me in the same way."

From that point forward, my mom made real progress with making herself more emotionally available to my kids and me. Another key part of her healing was having to care for my grandmother, who now has dementia. Seeing her mother in a helpless mental state and realizing that her father was still the same man he has always been caused my mother to take a look within herself. She realized that she had been wasting so much time with unresolved hurts that she was in danger of ending up like her parents. Who would want to end up miserable like my grandfather? Who would want to come to the end of life like my grandmother, who went through hell for her security only to have no control over it since she now has dementia?

My mom started her healing process and let go of everything her parents had done and allowed. Although healing is a forever process, the ground work has finally been laid for my mother at 50-plus years of age. She is now more present in my life and her grandkids' lives than ever. She is making genuine efforts to be a better mother, grandmother, and person. We talk more than ever now. I feel so close to her, and it is beautiful to see her ooze love and peace for the first time. It took her being transparent, owning her past and letting it go, and letting me in so that I could support her through it properly. I am so happy for her and look forward to sharing in the remainder of her life's journey with her.

CHAPTER 14:

Concrete Rose

AS I MENTIONED EARLIER IN this book, my cousin Sharon and I have been close since we were born. Her father is Uncle Ellis. I witnessed the turmoil in their household when I was around them, but I couldn't imagine what her life was like when I wasn't visiting. Her parents' tumultuous marriage and the mistreatment of her siblings were bound to have a negative effect on her, and they did via false friends, bad relationships, low-self-esteem and other negative events.

Sharon and her siblings were taught to mask the pain and put up a façade to hide the horrible things going on at home. Although everyone knew that her dad was abusing them and their mom, the family still felt the need to pretend everything was okay when it wasn't. Well, actually they did it to keep Sharon's father from harming them and their mother further; so, they had to play whatever role he wanted. The masking of pain and pretending became an art for them, so much so that it created in all of them a false sense of self—no true identity. Their identities were wrapped up in trying to get through the day without further abuse from their father or husband.

I mentioned the issue of colorism earlier. Sharon believes that the abuse her mother and sister suffered from her father was because their skin tone was lighter than other members of her immediate family. Since she had dark skin, Sharon believes my Uncle Ellis saw her as unattractive and less than, which she believed saved her from the physical and sexual abuse the women in her life suffered. That sounds crazy, but it's true. He sees lighter skinned women as objects and wants to control them in any way. It doesn't make sense, but much of what abusers do and think makes little sense.

Sharon used performing arts as way to escape from her home life. Rehearsals and shows began to occupy most of her time. Once she graduated high school, she went off to college. Like the rest of us, college for Sharon was the time during which she found herself and explored romantic relationships. Of course, the guys she dated were toxic for her. She was unable to appreciate the ones who actually meant well. Due to her traumatic upbringing, she didn't know how to receive and accept love fully. More than anything, Sharon didn't know how to love herself. The guys she sought out were broken individuals, too. Imagine two broken things trying to take the pieces of one another and put them back together. Those broken things can't help but end up with a mess on their hands. At least if one person is whole he or she can assist the other with healing…if the two are the right persons for each other to begin with. When a person is hurting, and running from past hurts and traumas, he or she will turn to things like drugs, sex, alcohol, material things, career, or anything in effort to fill those gaping voids instead of dealing with the primary issue. Running and faking gets exhausting after a while.

Outside of toxic relationships, Sharon was always the victim in her circumstances, no matter what. She would give every excuse why she didn't do something she set out to do, give every reason why things didn't work out in her favor, and she generally had a "woe is me" (learned helplessness) attitude about everything. She tended to embody the negative personality traits of the toxic guy she was dating at the time. She would reflect whatever that man thought of her since she didn't have an identity of her own. It hurts to see someone you love on such a downward spiral and doing things that you know do not represent the beautiful and precious person you cherish. My beloved cousin was allowing guys to treat her like crap because, well, at least they weren't beating on her in the manner that she witnessed happen to her mom. They tore down her self-esteem, confidence, and what little sense of self she had. In her mind, that was acceptable because it was better than being beaten. She attracted the wrong types of people, not only in romantic relationships, but also in friendships.

Your healing is important to every area of your life because if you don't heal, you are building your life on a foundation of hurt with no stability in that at all. Eventually it will all crumble.

Sharon finally grew tired of being mistreated after a rocky relationship and she and I actually had a falling out over her erratic behavior. Out of love, I begged and demanded that she get counseling. I made the appointment for her and even took her to her first counseling session. Sometimes you have to do that with people that you love. Your loved one can't always see how bad things are getting because he or she is in the situation. You may have to push that loved one in the right direction and force him or her to get the necessary help. Your heartfelt effort may not always work, but in this case, it did.

She stopped making excuses, stopped playing the victim, and made a choice to change her life. She attended counseling consistently, began going to church, focused on her writing and poetry, and started seeing herself in a healthy way. It was amazing to see her on her journey to wholeness. Her new path started with a decision and a support system.

Now Sharon is finishing up her first children's book, excelling in her career, is emotionally healthy, confident, and in the process, has met a man who treats her like a queen.

You can do it, too! Healing is yours for the taking, if you want it. Make the decision to stop the chaos in your life. Decide to live the fruitful life that you deserve.

Right now, you may not believe that a beautiful thing can emerge from the crazy life that you have, but nothing could be further from the truth. Don't believe the negative voices, people, or circumstances in your life. You have the power to change it. In the 21st century, we all have unlimited access to life-changing help. You have instant access through Google! If you don't have someone you can lean on in your personal life, you can find out about the hotlines and free and affordable counselors who are waiting to assist you on your path toward personal freedom.

Don't feel any guilt, shame, or embarrassment regarding your circumstances. Everyone has experienced his or her own version of hell. Allow the hurt to make you better by healing and learning from it. Most importantly, once you heal, pass that healing on, and help someone who needs it to get through his or her stuff.

SPOT REMOVAL RECAP

Journal Time!

In this section, we discussed turning points in my life and the lives of others that sparked their healing. Let's dig in and determine yours and your next steps.

1. Describe in detail the turning point in your life that made you want to take the first steps toward healing.
2. What areas are you struggling with in your journey toward healing?
3. What things are you finding hard to let go of?
4. Is there anything (even if it's within you) that is holding you back from healing completely? How do plan to move forward to stay on the right track?

SEVERING THE TIE AND DISCARDING THE HAND-ME-DOWNS

I have defined generational curses and soul ties, identified them, and shared stories of those who have overcome them. Now it is time for you to partake in the healing and finally rid yourself of what has had you bound.

CHAPTER 15:

Documentation

I REMEMBER WHEN MY Uncle Matt asked me "what will make you happy?" At that point, I really didn't know and couldn't answer that question. He instructed me to write down the things that made me unhappy. Don't worry; that will be a part of your journal exercise at the end of this section. After writing down those things, I then had to jot down my list of things that I believed would personally make me happy. Additionally, he also had me ponder where my pride originated from and how it has affected me with specific examples (like having material possessions, career/academic advancements, and feeling like I couldn't depend on a man, to name a few). He then had me write down how to rid myself of my pride.

Now these tasks seem simple; in fact, they are until you actually have to write them down and think about them. I was stuck initially trying to figure out exactly what would make me happy. My pride is what developed as a result of everything I endured growing up. At first, pride helped me, or so it seemed, but of course it started to work against me. It is no wonder then, that I got to the point of having post-partum depression and struggling with my identity.

Writing is an important part of healing, in my opinion. Writing things down cleanses you and forces you to face issues that you otherwise wouldn't be able to handle. It gives you the platform to organize your thoughts and let things flow from the heart.

I know what you are thinking: you're not a writer, or you don't have anything to write about. I said the same about myself, but a key part of healing is getting face to face with those issues. Writing helps make things real and gives you clarity that you wouldn't have by just thinking or talking about it. Having things written down also gives you a tangible reminder of what you are working towards. I write my long and short term goals down every few months, pray over them, do everything I can on my end to make it work, and revisit my list to check my progress. Trust me; it helps. Also, when the healing process hurts or you feel yourself slipping back into negative ways, you can always revisit your journal. Revisiting helps remind you of where you are trying to go and forces you to remember important details about the life you are trying to abandon. Taking the time to write out my frustrations, listing where I was in my journey in contrast to where I wanted to be, and reviewing what I had written often helped me finally pull the curses by the root from my life and discard them. I had to do the same for the soul tie that I discussed.

Once I was finally done with that relationship and realized that I was still suffering from it spiritually and in other ways I sought the help of the psychologist with whom I was working as an intern at the time. I told her about all of the demonic attacks that I was having, and luckily, she didn't hit me with any psychobabble to make me feel crazy. She gave me the number of one of her good friends. I spoke with her friend, who invited me to her church. Now I do believe in prophets and those who have spiritual gifts. I have gifts myself and you do, too. I was led to a woman at that church who spoke to me as a messenger from God. I knew she was His messenger because she spoke to me about things I hadn't shared with anyone else. She spoke about them to me matter-of-factly, thus confirming for me that throughout my entire journey of hell, He was there all along. My next thought was, *Lord where have you been all this time.*

At this church, I learned how to take authority over the demonic forces that had held me hostage for some time. I was so frightened by my experiences that I couldn't operate in my God-given authority. How do you get to a place of operating in your God-given authority, you ask? You have to believe truly that these attacks are not a form of punishment. They don't have to be literal demonic attacks, either. Your attacks may be in the form of anxiety, worry, stress, fear, or other debilitating challenges. Once you remove the "woe is me," helpless attitude, you can begin to see things a bit clearer. Replace helplessness with the confidence and power to get through anything through Christ.

Again, this is how I was able to get through *my* mess, and I hope that you are able to get through yours as well. I had to write down *and* say I what I wanted to see. I had to write down and claim that I had authority over the issues that plagued me. I had to declare that I was free of them. After I wrote my affirmations down, I would say them aloud every day and believe what I was saying. At the end of this section, I will show you examples of affirmations so that you can create your own. I also included scriptures in my affirmations and made them personal. I will show you examples of that as well.

Since I was having literal demonic attacks via the soul tie I had in my life, I also anointed my place. I am a big advocate of anointing wherever I may reside. I use regular olive oil, pray over it, touch everything in my home with it, declare aloud that everything is blessed and protected, and rebuke all evil forces because none should dwell where you live. Here is how rebuking looks. Let's say that I am feeling negative energy of some sort hovering over me (like the feeling of emotional heaviness). I would then start speaking out loud something along the lines of "In the name of Jesus, I rebuke any feelings of anxiety, fear, worry, or heaviness. These things have no place in my life, and I am covered in the blood of Jesus. I command these negative feelings to flee from me in the name of Jesus." I would keep repeating it until I feel peace.

It works.

Speaking over your life in a positive way is important. The Bible talks about speaking over your life and the power of the tongue (see Proverbs 18:2, Mark 11:22-24). This concept is always in line with the laws of attraction. All you are doing is proclaiming what you want. Remember, we are spirit beings in the physical realm, so you have to be aware of the things that are unseen even more than you are aware of the things that are seen.

I am able to feel when a demonic attack is coming on. If you are having them, you have to get up and call those forces into submission right then and there. I have had to wake up and literally command demons to flee. For example, I would say something like

"In the name of Jesus, Satan, I command you to leave my home. I bind and rebuke this attack in the name of Jesus." If I was already asleep and caught off guard by the attack, I would call on the name of Jesus and once I was free from the hold I would speak the prayer that I said above and roll back over peacefully. It's rare for me now, but if I feel anxious while I am asleep, I start repeating Psalm 3:24. I say "as I lie down, my sleep will be sweet" over and over and before I know it, I am sleeping peacefully. There is nothing new to the tools that I am sharing. They are all a part of the law of attraction—having what you say and thinking what you want to be and see happen in your life. These tools as I have shown them to you here include my personal spin to combat generational curses and soul ties.

As I dealt with the soul tie itself, I had to pray a prayer daily until I felt whole. If you want, you can do a seven-day fast as well. Fasts assist you with spiritual clarity. So, as you purge this tie from your life, you give yourself the peace your spirit has been craving. When you choose to fast, you are usually abstaining from things that you find pleasurable or distracting. It can be sex, social media, certain foods (or food period once you do the necessary research to ensure you remain healthy), or gossip, to offer a few examples. Only *you* know the things that are distractions for you or what you consider to be pleasurable to determine what you would fast from. My own prayer went like this:

"Father God, I thank you for saving me from destruction. I praise you for sending Jesus to die for my sins. Please forgive me for my sins against you. Specifically, I confess that I _____(details and names of the sins). I repent of that sin and renounce it now. Lord, please purify my heart from this sin, the memory of it, and any associated fantasy I have entertained in my mind regarding it. In the name of Jesus Christ and by the power of his blood shed on the cross, I cut myself free from any soul ties that may have been established with _____ (name (s) or specific objects). I commit him/her/them to the care of Jesus Christ for him to do with as he wills. Satan, I rebuke you in all your works and ways. I rebuke any evil spirits that have a foothold in me. In the name of Jesus, I command you, evil spirits, to leave me and go directly to Jesus Christ. Father, please heal my soul of any wounds resulting from these soul ties. Please reintegrate any part of me that may have been damaged through this/these soul ties and restore me to wholeness. I also ask that you reintegrate any part of the person(s) I sinned with that has been detached in me, and restore them to wholeness. Thank you, Lord, for your healing power and your perfect love for me. May I glorify you with my life from this point forward. In Jesus' name, Amen."

(http://www.missionariesofprayer.org/2010/11/prayer-cut-soul-ties/, 2016).

You can use this exact prayer and fill it in or tweak it so that it is exactly what you need. I am thankful that I stumbled across the blog I have cited above after discovering and identifying that the demonic attacks I was going through were the result of a soul tie.

So, those are the spiritual things that I had to do to sever the soul tie. I also had to get rid of anything that was tied to where the soul tie came from. It can be anything: clothes, gifts, texts, phone numbers, emails, or social media accounts. Dump it ALL. You have to purge yourself from all of the nonsense and not reopen the doors in any way. Otherwise, your efforts will be null and void.

CHAPTER 16:

Facing the Demons

IN SOME SITUATIONS, IT IS important to talk to the people who caused the hurt in your life. Not all situations will allow you to talk directly with the person; he or she may have passed on, or it is not safe to contact the person. So, writing a raw letter without holding anything back will also work. The main person in my life whom I had to face was my grandfather. He was the source of the majority of my pain.

In December 2014, I called my grandfather about something and somehow, as was normal for our interactions, we ended up in an argument where I felt I had to check him. I refused to deal with his disrespect and he insisted on testing me, so a blowout between us was inevitable. For whatever reason, this argument was no different than our many others, but I felt incredibly heavy after I hung up the phone on him. I told my Uncle Matt how I was feeling and didn't know what to do to rid myself of the exhaustion I was feeling from arguing with my grandfather.

I decided that enough was enough and it was finally time to tell him why I was always so combative toward him. I had to tell him that the reason I have such anger with him is because I watched him mistreat my grandmother, verbally and sometimes physically abusing her, as well as groping, fondling, and forcing himself onto my mother as I watched, helpless and confused, as a child.

This confrontation was a major step for me. I was scared and didn't even know what would happen if I finally told him the truth. However, I didn't have a choice. I was tired of being angry; I was tired of my own attitude; and I felt imprisoned to myself because of what I saw as a child. I wanted to be free. I prayed and asked God to guide my words and help me through that conversation and that his ears would actually be open to truly hear me. Anytime I have to do anything difficult, especially when I have to have a hard conversation, I always ask God to help me and give me courage and the right words to say.

So a few days later, I finally had my mind right and called my grandfather. I was shaken up, scared, and near tears. I had to literally push myself not to punk out and hang up the phone. I started the conversation and said "Do you know how you are always talking about how I have a bad attitude, well I need to tell you why that is." From there, I told him what I saw him do in detail as child growing up in his house and how his actions had completely ruined my life. I couldn't hold back the tears while talking to him because it hurt so bad to finally tell him, but I also felt so free. It was definitely a bittersweet moment for me. To my surprise, he didn't deny anything I said. He actually owned his stuff 100%. I was in total shock. I told him that I forgave him and he apologized. He said "Deb, I didn't know that you saw all of that. I have had so many demons to battle in my life, and I don't know why I've done the things I've done."

That was good enough for me coming from this man, because I didn't even expect him to hold himself accountable. From that moment forward, the weight was lifted off me. The primary culprit of my generational issues now knew what he had done. Now I could move forward. Even if his reaction had been a bad one, I would've still been free because I forgave him, so I am no longer held hostage by his actions. Now, although I am free from his actions that scarred me long ago and I forgive him, HE has not changed the person he is. As I mentioned before, he STILL mistreats and disrespects my grandmother and communicates poorly with everyone around him. There is considerable distance between my grandfather and me because he is just not someone who allows anyone to get close to him. My conversation with him and decision to forgive him was solely for me and my sanity. If he had taken that as an opportunity to change that would have been a plus, but he refuses to be anything other than what he has always been. Again, forgiveness and confronting the issues are milestones for the person doing the forgiving and confronting most times. At the end of this lesson, there will be an activity to help you face the demons in your own life.

CHAPTER 17:

Iron Sharpens Iron

THE NEXT THING YOU MUST DO is talk through what you have gone through with someone you trust and who is your voice of reason. If you don't have such a person in your life, you should seek the services of a professional counselor. Bouncing your experiences off of someone else will allow you to be free of the situation by verbally affirming that you no longer have to be bound by your past. Talking through the issue also requires whoever you choose to share your story with to be an accountability partner. When this person sees you slipping back into your old ways, he or she can call you out and get you back on your path toward healing. He or she can also cheer you on as you make your changes.

Now, with that said please make sure that whoever you trust to go along with you on your healing journey is actually a TRUE friend. Is he or she loyal? Have you detected any issues of jealousy? Is your best interest at the person's heart? Is he or she honest with you, or does this person tell you what you want to hear? Are your certain the person is of sound mind? Is he or she mature and unbiased? These are just a few questions to ask yourself when determining who to select if you don't have anyone yet. Before engaging in this accountability exercise, ask God to give you discernment and remove from your life those who should no longer be in your life because those people bring you down and continue to feed the very curses that you are trying to break.

I have several accountability partners I can count on to get me together and keep my head on straight. When I am overthinking things, they reassure me. When I am being a nut job, they let me know that I have lost my mind. Iron truly sharpens iron. If our relationships aren't making us better, then they are making us worse. I am speaking more to those in your close circle. Who is in your close circle of trusted people? Do they add to you? Are you adding to them?

Support and accountability are crucial during the healing process. Whether you receive help from a counselor, friend, partner, or family member, you need someone else to help you get through this. Surrounding yourself with genuine or people will make your healing process much smoother, even while it is still a painful process. We were not meant to go through our life journeys alone. We need others to help us get through life and we also have to use our situations to bless someone with the nuggets you have learned to get through theirs. Now is not the time for "yes men" or people who will allow you to continue in a downward spiral. If they aren't pushing you forward, they are holding you back...period.

This would also be a great time to identify your relationships with others and start distancing yourself from and weeding out those who are not good for you. I don't care if it's a family member, friend you've had since kindergarten, or your mom (I am serious). If someone is contributing to your physical, spiritual, and emotional demise, that person has to go. If someone in your life is enabling you to continue your destructive behavior, that person is also a big part of your problem. Failure to call you out and hold you accountable is also a form of reinforcing your dose of poison, thus keeping you stuck.

Is this harsh? Yup!

However, your life depends on your healing, and someone else's life depends on your healing as well.

A friend of mine was hitting a brick wall in all of her relationships, from her romantic relationship to her friendships. She realized she was not getting what she needed emotionally from any of us. We had no clue that she needed anything at all. She is extremely sweet and funny, but she also keeps to herself and doesn open up about personal matters. At the moment of her breakdown, she wept as she noted that she felt out of the loop on what was going on within our circle of friends. Every time she expressed how she felt, she would then say, "but it's no big deal." That was an immediate red flag to all of us, so we used her moment of vulnerability to force her to express herself in a safe place. We also encouraged her and let her know that her feelings were valid and important to all of us.

Your feelings are valid! *Yes, yours!* Don't continue to brush your feelings off as no big deal. They ARE a big deal. Believe it!

After that day, my friend and I began talking to help get to the root of her heartache and hindrances in relationships. We were led to discuss her romantic relationship first. Of course, I asked about her childhood and her family. Through our discussion, I learned that her father would constantly talk down to and demean her mother. At first, she wanted to downplay how her father treated her mom by saying "he never hit her or anything, so it wasn't that bad." From there, I showed her that verbal or emotional abuse is still abuse. From watching her parents, she grew to believe that her feelings weren't valid and could be shot down at any moment. This belief was at the root of why she never got too personal or expressed her real feelings with us. On the flip side, she became her father in her romantic relationship. She used the belittling, passive, controlling, and harsh tongue that was used against her mother against her own significant other. From that point, we were able to start uprooting the real issues that were holding her back so that she would have freedom from all of her issues in all of her relationships.

My friend's path toward healing is an example of why it is crucial to have genuine people in your life who care about you in all aspects. If the people in our circle of friends were self-consumed, we would not have been able to recognize how much she needed us; we would not have known that she was crying out for help without her actually saying it. We hold her accountable to her healing now, and also make sure we affirm that she matters and that she has a voice within our group.

Now, how does someone else's healing depend on yours? Nothing—and I mean NOTHING—that we ever go through is for ourselves. Every trial and tribulation is essentially to help the next person. All of the hell I have been through and witnessed is helping you now, isn't it? If I hadn't had an abortion in college, miscarried two children, had a failed business, had crappy relationships, or made mistakes, I would not be able to keep others from slipping into the same pitfalls or give others the tools they need to push through to success in their life journeys. Now, I am not saying that your life's goal should be to suffer. However, we all will always have both good days and bad. We don't need a guide to live through the good moments because that is the easy part of living. Sometimes those hard moments can make it hard for you to see the good that is going on in your life because the stress robs you of peace. When things are peaceful and carefree, they are just that. It is when things become difficult and you begin dealing with resistance from life, that things become hard to handle.

Everyone needs someone to help him or her get through his or her problems or at least provide them with the tools to know how to do so. If you learn nothing else from this book, I hope that you can take what you have learned and use it to heal yourself and bless someone else. Even if you are still going through and in the process of healing, you still have what it takes to pass the techniques for healing to someone else. To help someone else who is going through although you have a lot going on yourself is always a true test of character. However, offering this help is not supposed to drain you; self-care is priority. If you do not feel strong enough to help someone else, then don't do it. It is my personal belief that helping others despite your current circumstance is also helpful to you. You know that you are strong enough when you are able to be unbiased, objective, and sensitive to the other person's needs. Sometimes God gives us strength to encourage others that we don't realize that we have in those moments that present themselves. If you see someone going through a situation that you know all too well, do take the opportunity to encourage that person and be transparent with him or her. You will find blessing someone else will help you heal as well. Being closed off and self-consumed will only make your problems appear that much bigger and will also cause a delay in your healing. To paraphrase an old and often-used saying, step out of the forest so that you can see the trees. Giving someone else the gift of peace and freedom is invaluable, both to the person receiving the gift and to the giver of the gift.

It is important that you are completely transparent and open throughout your healing process. You never want to give yourself an opportunity to hide or create a false sense of self regarding your experiences. If you do, you will surely delay your healing and remain trapped. Transparency is critical to moving forward because you are no longer allowing your past to pull the strings in your life. Once you own it then it can no longer hold you hostage. It's like being picked on in school for being overweight or having buck teeth. Did you notice that the kids who were targeted for their prominent flaws were left alone after they stood up to their bullies and owned whatever "flaw" they had? In the simplest form, that is exactly how most personal issues are tackled. That personal issue can be insecurity, anxiety, or abuse. Face it head on and use your team of support to keep you grounded. Being out in the open with your problems may be terrifying, but it will give you the courage to overcome all of the things that have kept you trapped.

CHAPTER 18:

Laying it at the Father's Feet

LASTLY, **PRAY.** PRAYER AND meditation are what will seal the deal for you in your healing journey, but only if you **believe** that they will. I am constantly leaning on God to help me through every part of my life. No part of my healing journey excluded prayer. I had to pray because sometimes I was so isolated while going through; and prayer was all I had. I have had so many personal encounters with Him that I would be remiss not to acknowledge Him. If you don't have a personal relationship with Him and if you want to take that next step, there is no time like the present to do so. It doesn't matter what you've done, what you've been through, or how you feel. There will never be a perfect time, and you don't need to have it together in order to come to Him.

I can't give any true instructions on how to do so because it is YOUR relationship with Him and not mine. However, if you want to seek God from a Christian perspective, please read John 3:16 in the Bible: "For God so loved the world, that he gave his only begotten Son, that whosoever believeth on him should not perish, but have eternal life. For God so loved the world, that He gave His only begotten Son, that whoever believes in Him should not perish, but have eternal life." From there, you can pray and ask God to come into your heart and confess Jesus as your Lord and Savior. Again, there is no pressure; do what is right for you. You are the determining factor of where your relationship with God goes and whether to start it. As a matter of fact, let's get you started with a closing/beginning prayer for your journey. The choice is yours! Go get your healing:

Heavenly Father,

Thank you for leading me to this book. Thank you that the generational curses and soul ties in my life and in the lives of others have been broken. Father, I want a relationship with You and I need Your help to heal. Give me the courage, boldness, and strength to conquer my healing. Show me the weak areas of my life and build them up. Remove those people and things that should no longer be a part of my life and replace them with those that should. Unshackle me from all the things that are holding me back. I bind and rebuke any assignments or missions that the enemy has placed on my life and in the lives of my loved ones. Let the curses end with me. Help me to pass the healing on to others. I need You and I submit myself to the will you have for my life. Don't let me give up. In Jesus Name, Amen!

SEVERING THE TIE AND DISCARDING THE HAND-ME-DOWNS RECAP

Journal Time!

In the final section, we have gone over ways that are sure to assist you in your healing journey if you are committed to it. Let's create your healing plan.

1. What will make you happy? Be completely honest and list the things that you feel will make you truly happy. It doesn't matter how silly you may think a thing is, write it down. This is for *you*. You are creating your goal list.

2. What has been making you miserable?

3. What are the things that have held you back from healing the way you should? List these.

4. Based on the two lists that you have created and the information given in this last section, how can you achieve the happiness that you seek? This will be your action list.

5. Who are your accountability partners? By what date will you share with them what your plan is and what you need from them to help you?

6. Write a detailed letter to the person, people, or things (yes, things) that have hurt you. If you feel comfortable and if it is possible, give the person or people that letter to let them know how you feel, or call them on the phone. If you would rather keep those feelings between you and the paper, that is okay, too. After you are done, rip it up, and discard it. Destroying the unsent letter will be symbolic that you have released all of the hurt and are done with it having control of your life.

7. If you are also ridding yourself of a soul tie, have you started the process of severing that tie based on the suggestions I mentioned earlier? What have you done or what will you do? By what date will this be done?

8. Have you prayed about your healing process? Have you asked God to help you and strengthen you in the areas in which you feel weak? If not, write an honest prayer of what you need from him and believe that it is done for you in Jesus's name.

9. Continue to revisit your action and goal lists to check your progress and determine your next steps. Don't give up!

APPENDIX:
ADDITIONAL READING

"The Willie Lynch Letter," mentioned on page 2." Source: http://www.finalcall.com/artman/publish/Perspectives_1/Willie_Lynch_letter_The_Making_of_a_Slave.shtml

Prayer to Cut Soul Ties, mentioned on page 77. (http://www.missionariesofprayer.org/2010/11/prayer-cut-soul-ties/, 2016).

Made in the USA
Monee, IL
07 July 2020